NORTH YORKSHIRE

OFF THE BEATEN TRACK

Eileen Rennison

with illustrations by
Philip Rennison

COUNTRYSIDE BOOKS
NEWBURY BERKSHIRE

First published 2003
© Eileen Rennison 2003

COUNTRYSIDE BOOKS
3 Catherine Road
Newbury, Berkshire

To view our complete range of books,
please visit us at
www.countrysidebooks.co.uk

ISBN 1 85306 804 7

Front cover photograph of Pen-y-Ghent
near Horton-in-Ribblesdale
supplied by Bill Meadows

Designed by Graham Whiteman

Produced through MRM Associates Ltd., Reading
Typeset by Mac Style Ltd, Scarborough, N. Yorkshire
Printed by J.W. Arrowsmith Ltd., Bristol

INTRODUCTION

North Yorkshire, the administrative county created in the reorganisation of boundaries in 1974, and the largest county in England, covers an area of 803,741 hectares and stretches from the coast in the east to the Pennines in the west. It contains within its borders the North York Moors National Park (553 sq. m.), established in 1952, the Yorkshire Dales National Park (650 sq. m.), established two years later, and lying between the two the Vale of York. This large area has many attractive villages and small market towns but few cities of any great size. It is mostly rural, dependent in the main on farming and tourism.

This book will attempt to show to readers the many different facets of the county: its wealth of ancient castles, abbeys, churches and other places of historical, artistic and literary interest, as well as the astonishing variety of scenery. There are many more places than those featured equally worthy of note and excluded only through lack of space. Researching and writing this book has been an opportunity for me to take a closer look at an area that has long been familiar to me. I was born in a North Riding village and apart from a brief period after my marriage have lived in Yorkshire all my life, though not always in the North Riding. (And yes – the Ridings do still exist.)

Details build up to give a bigger picture and if we know where and how to look we can learn much about the past. Even small details can offer us insights into the way people lived and worked, their ideas and attitudes, their folklore and customs. We realise the dominance here in Yorkshire of certain powerful families in the past, understand the part played by the Church in establishing sheep farming, cheese-making, horse breeding and agriculture – all still prominent in the area today – and learn that the dales and moors, valued today for their scenic beauty, were once centres of lead, coal and ironstone mining.

Nature and man together have over thousands of years made North Yorkshire what it is today, and both will inevitably continue to have their effect. Our role now must surely be to conserve what we have, whilst accepting necessary changes and adapting them with sensitivity to the needs of the people who live here. North Yorkshire is an area like no other – though of course I would say that, wouldn't I! I must leave you to judge for yourself.

Eileen Rennison

MAP OF NORTH YORKSHIRE

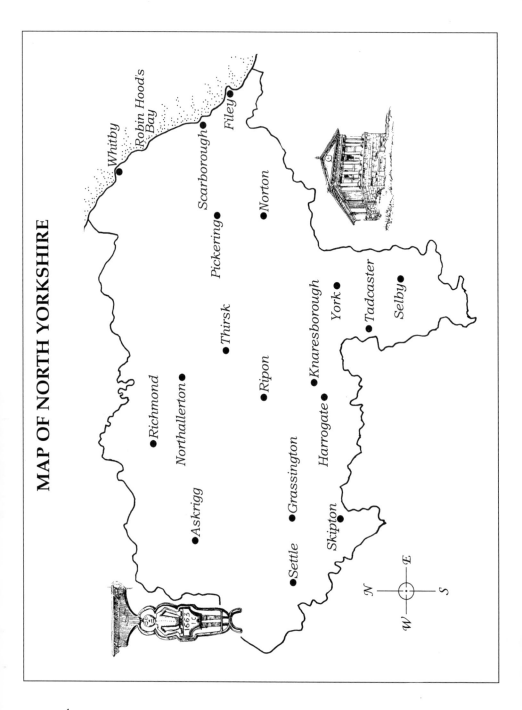

Whitby

Robin Hood's Bay

Scarborough

Filey

Norton

Pickering

Thirsk

Ripon

Richmond

Northallerton

Askrigg

Grassington

Settle

Skipton

Harrogate

Knaresborough

York

Tadcaster

Selby

1663

N E S W

ACASTER MALBIS *Grid ref. SE 587454*

Just beyond the archbishop's palace in the village of Bishopthorpe, near York, a road to the left is signed Acaster Airfield, the only remaining reminder of the Second World War airfield, which opened in 1942, closed in 1946 and is now used for agricultural purposes. Some two or three miles on, along the road that follows the course of the River Ouse, a left turn at the Ship Inn brings one into Acaster Malbis. It takes its name from the Malbys, who were granted land here after 1066, but long before that it was the site of a Roman fort. In medieval times the Archbishop of York probably followed much the same route from his palace beside – or even on – the river, for it is thought that he came here for contemplation and prayer in the ancient chapel of ease, now the village church. The manor house of 1700 at one time housed a private school and is now a hotel.

Being close to the river, the village is popular with boaters and caravanners, but in an earlier age that situation made it ideal for an unusual agricultural crop – peppermint. The plant (*Mentha piperita*) likes damp places and flowers from July to September with purple spikes rather like lavender. The leaves and flowering tops, gathered and dried when the flowers begin to open, are used to obtain peppermint oil, for use in medicine and confectionery. Peppermint is a well-used remedy for digestive problems and gives its flavour to many sweets. Nowadays it is produced mainly by the large-scale growers of America. The lands around Acaster Malbis must once however have been as lovely a sight as lavender fields are today in other parts of the country – and an aromatic delight to work in. A round, now rusty piece of the distillery equipment dating from about 1840, preserved behind the railings of a small building as one enters the village, is the only reminder of this one-time trade.

AINDERBY STEEPLE *Grid ref. SE 335920*

Three miles south-west of Northallerton, on a small hill in the Vale of York, is Ainderby Steeple – but, although the church tower is certainly very high, it has no steeple. It dates from the 15th century, and it may be that the church, much of which is earlier in date, once had a steeple, which gave its name to the village, thus distinguishing it from other Ainderbys in the area.

Richard Scrope, later to become Archbishop of York, was once the rector here. He was executed in 1405 for his part in the rebellion of the Earl of Northumberland against Henry IV, and earned for himself the title of the Martyr Archbishop. He was regarded even by his opponents as a man of the highest character.

In the early 1950s it was reported in the local paper that an apparition of a black-draped coffin, floating unsupported and followed by an archbishop silently reading from a prayer book, had been seen by the residents of Clementhorpe, now an area of York, but once in open countryside. According to local legend it is the ghost of Archbishop Scrope, who was executed near that spot, and it has reputedly been seen from time to time over the years.

ALDBOROUGH   *Grid ref. SE 407664*

As Iseur, Aldborough was the capital of the powerful Brigantes tribe. Later, the Romans established a camp there, and as *Isurium Brigantum* it was an important Romano-British town, linked by road to York (*Eboracum*) and to Hadrian's Wall to the north. Tesselated pavements and other Roman remains have been excavated and can be seen in the museum there. Other remains are known to exist under houses in the village.

On a small area of grass near the church and close by a little timbered cottage is a tall clustered column, obviously of great age, with an unusual top of acanthus-like leaves. There is nothing to indicate its purpose, but it has been suggested that it commemorates the Battle of Boroughbridge in 1322, when Edward II defeated the Earl of Lancaster.

Today Aldborough is almost part of Boroughbridge, its very near neighbour, but this delightful village is steeped in history and was once an important and significant place in its own right.

ALDWARK   *Grid ref. SE 468637*

All the materials for St Stephen's church, built between 1846 and 1853 at Aldwark, were brought, appropriately, to the site by river, for it stands beside the River Ure, close to the point where the Swale and the Ure join the River Ouse. The result is a very quaint and pretty little church; with its high pitched roof and walls of herringbone brickwork intermingled with stones and flints, it has an almost fairytale appearance, a suggestion of the gingerbread house in Hansel and Gretel, perhaps.

The river in the past was an important means of transport, used certainly as far back as Roman times and into the 20th century to carry the produce of the area down to York, and coal and other necessities to villages upstream such as Aldwark. Only with the coming of the railways did the river traffic decline.

Behind the church, the river is crossed by a toll bridge. Both toll bridges and toll roads were once common, but most tolls were abolished by 1895. Before roads and bridges became the responsibility of the county authorities, their building and maintenance fell to first individual parishes and then, in the 17th century, to the turnpike trusts, which recouped their costs by charging all who used them. Bridges at Selby and Cawood in North Yorkshire which were previously toll bridges eventually became free, leaving the bridge across the Ure at Aldwark the only remaining toll bridge in the area. It was built by farmers for their convenience, and was managed by the National Farmers' Union until it was sold to a private owner. The keeper at the little white toll house is kept very busy collecting the money and issuing tickets to the accompaniment of the clatter of the bridge's wooden slats as the vehicles pass over.

ALNE   *Grid ref. SE 497654*

This is a village whose name causes a problem for many people. How does one pronounce it? Just say *awn* to rhyme with *dawn* and you can't go wrong. There are many theories as to how it came by its name. One suggestion gives the alder trees in the area the credit for its origin, but nobody really knows.

In the grass verge at the crossroads from which one turns down The Avenue into the village is a small stone, said to be the remains of a plague stone erected in 1604. At the base of the upright stone is a small trough into which money could be placed in some form of disinfectant, possibly vinegar, as payment for goods left there. In this way, direct contact with villagers who might be carrying infection was avoided.

At the bottom of the hill, a bridge crosses the little River Kyle and on the right is Alne Hall, now a Cheshire Home. Alne has two halls. At the opposite end of the village, near the old railway station, is Low Hall.

A little further on, the church of St Mary is testimony to the long history of the village. The top half of the tower is of brick, but a Viking stone can be seen above the chancel doorway and there are many indications of Norman origin. The most splendid of these is the south door arch, which has a double row of unique carved animals and figures. Though sadly eroded with age, it is still possible to recognise some of them. The inner order is of animals and birds, but includes a man slaughtering a pig. The creatures in the outer order are interpretations of medieval manuscripts. The bird looking at a man represents the white bird which is said to look at a sick man if he is to recover or to turn

The maiden's crants, St Mary's church, Alne.

away if he is to die. A fox playing dead to catch unwary birds symbolises the Devil, out to catch men's souls.

Also in the church is a sad little relic of an old custom: a coronet of paper flowers, yellowed with age, known as a 'maiden's crants'. The word, used by Shakespeare, means 'garland' – like the German word *Kranz*. It was carried by two girls before the coffin of an unmarried maiden and placed afterwards in the church. This example dates from the beginning of the 18th century and is one of the few that survive. A stone effigy in the chapel is thought to be of Lady Ellerker from nearby Youlton Hall, who built the chapel in the 14th century. A modern window in the church brings us nearer to our own time. It replaces one blown out during the last war, when a loaded bomber crashed soon after take-off from a nearby airfield.

Beyond the church is the old two-roomed school, now the village hall. The road alongside it has the unusual and intriguing name of Jack Hole.

The broad main street, with grass verges on either side, has houses and cottages set in very long gardens, both to front and back. There were once two thatched cottages in the village, but though one remains it is no longer thatched and the other has been demolished.

A road leading off to the right takes one back to Alne Hall. The road's ancient name of Monk Green has a medieval sound to it, a reminder of some long ago monastic connection. It is a shady tree-lined spot, where despite some modern building it is still possible to imagine a monk strolling in religious contemplation.

At the far end of the village, where once was the village pond, is now a grassy area, on which a number of trees have been planted in memory of past inhabitants.

Before the Second World World War Alne had three general stores, a post office, a butcher's shop, a cobbler's, a joiner and undertaker's, a blacksmith's and three public houses: the Blue Bell, the Fox and Goose and the Station Hotel. Today only one small combined shop and post office, the joiner and undertaker's and the Blue Bell pub remain. Despite these changes, it is a thriving and forward-looking community. But then, a village named in Domesday Book will have survived many changes over the centuries!

AMPLEFORTH *Grid ref. SE 585785*

In 1802 the Benedictine monks came over from France and built their great abbey at Ampleforth. Six years later, with only four pupils, they opened the school which is today the famous Catholic public school, and for many synonymous with the name Ampleforth. The village, however, existed long before the coming of the monks. It was an early Anglo-Saxon settlement recorded in 1086 in the Domesday Book as *Ampreforde*, which means 'ford of the sorrel plant'. To the north of the village, surrounded by dykes and ditches, is a Bronze Age fort known as Studford Ring, which can be reached by public footpath.

In 1940 Ampleforth became home and haven to the famous Viennese sculptor Josef Heu, a refugee from the Nazis, who fled with his family to England. They were warmly welcomed into the community and he worked with the woodcarver known as 'Mousey' Thompson in the nearby village of Kilburn, at the foot of the Hambleton Hills. Examples of his work are to be seen in many village churches in the area. The wooden statue of the Virgin and Child in St Benedict's church in Ampleforth was carved by him in 1947. The Christ Child, cradled in his mother's arms holds a ball in his hands symbolising the globe and reminding us that God created the world and holds all within his hands.

APPLETON-LE-MOORS *Grid ref. SE 735875*

A single main street with back lanes, the northern end with views of the moors and the southern end looking down to the Vale of Pickering – this is Appleton-le-Moors, a typical moorland village of stone-built houses and grazing sheep, tucked just within the southern boundary of the North York Moors National Park. Up here the air is wonderfully fresh and the views outstanding, those to the south stretching across miles, as far even as the Wolds in East Yorkshire.

The village owes much to Joseph Shepherd. He was born in Appleton of poor parents, but left to go to sea. He became prosperous in the whaling business, for which the Yorkshire coast was an important centre at the time. Having made his

Three faces, Appleton-le-Moors.

fortune, he returned to his native village in the 1850s and built himself a grand villa – Appleton Hall – now a hotel. He was determined to use his wealth to benefit the local inhabitants, and in particular to provide the children with the education that he had never had. Sadly he died in 1862 before he was able to carry out his plans, and it fell to his widow to fulfil his dreams. She built the village school and schoolhouse, and then she commissioned the architect J.L. Pearson – who later built Truro Cathedral – to build, at a cost of £10,000, the ornately decorated church whose tall tower and spire can be seen for miles across the moors. Wall paintings in the Shepherd memorial chapel show Biblical scenes relating to the sea, in acknowledgement of the source of the benefactor's wealth, while the windows depict the Acts of Mercy.

On a cottage in the main street are three faces carved in stone, which tell a less charitable story. They are said to represent the Three Bloodsuckers, a satirical portrayal of lawyer, doctor, and clergyman, though there is nothing to tell us which is which. See for yourself and decide!

ASKRIGG *Grid ref. SD 945915*

The grey stone village of Askrigg in Wensleydale, perched 800 feet above sea level, may be familiar to television viewers, though perhaps they do not recognise it by that name. It became Darrowby as the location for the filming of the popular series *All Creatures Great and Small*. The house in the market square, now renamed Skeldale House, was the home and the surgery of the fictional vet James Herriot.

Although there were settlements here from very early times, most of the present buildings are from the 18th and 19th centuries, when Askrigg was a centre of industries such as hand knitting, textiles and clock-making. There was also some lead mining in the area, and, when the mines began to fail in the 18th century, there were bread riots by the miners in the neighbourhood of Askrigg, resulting in some of the rioters being sent to the gallows. The knitting industry began in Askrigg in Elizabethan times. Hosiers travelled around the countryside distributing wool for spinning and knitting by people in their own homes. The pay was very poor – as little as one groat for knitting a jersey – and knitters were forced to knit all day long every day to earn a meagre living. In about 1785, a cotton mill was built at Askrigg, but it soon ceased to spin cotton, and turned to spinning wool into yarn for knitting and coarse cloth, thus reverting to the traditional industry.

The heyday of the Askrigg clock-makers was the 18th century. James Ogden, Mark Metcalfe and Christopher Caygill were three famous makers, producing curious designs and using unusual tools. Christopher Caygill often decorated his clock-faces with depictions of the Devil, though he sometimes included angels or the four evangelists.

The name of Metcalfe is a familiar one in this area even today, and Nappa Hall, east of Askrigg, was the home of the huge Metcalfe clan, which played a dominant part in Upper Wensleydale in the 16th and 17th centuries. In 1556, Sir Christopher Metcalfe, as High Sheriff of Yorkshire, rode out to meet the Assize Judges and escort them to York, together with 300 of his kinsmen, each and every one of whom was mounted on a white horse. The hall, built about 1475, with embattled towers and a grand porch, is regarded as one of the finest examples of early domestic architecture in Yorkshire. Today it is a farmhouse, but, according to tradition, both King James I and Mary, Queen of Scots stayed there.

Like many other market squares, Askrigg's was once the scene of the cruel sport of bull-baiting, and the stone for the ring, to which the animal was tethered, is still there.

AYSGARTH *Grid ref. SE 005885*

The striking landscape of Wensleydale is formed by the Yoredale series, the name given to the geological layers of shale, sandstone and limestone which, weathering and eroding at different rates, give the great bold scars and innumerable waterfalls that are characteristic of the dale. The most famous of the waterfalls are those at Aysgarth: Upper, Middle and Lower Falls, which cascade over rocky terraces in the River Ure, all within less than a mile of each other. The Upper Falls can be viewed from the Yore Bridge, built in the 16th century, while the Middle Falls are reached along a wooded footpath on the north bank of the river. The Lower Falls, further downstream, are considered by many to be the most spectacular, but are often overlooked by visitors.

When the river is full, rushing and tumbling over the tiers of limestone rocks, it is hard to believe that it could ever be otherwise, yet in summer drought it has been known to become completely dry. It has also been seen to go from a barely noticeable trickle to a rolling torrent within the space of two minutes, in response to a downpour up at the head of the dale. This sudden change is typical of the rivers in the Dales and it can be dangerous.

Since 1954 Aysgarth has had no railway station, but the falls owe their popularity, as with so many tourist attractions and beauty spots, to the accessibility afforded during the railway era. They were threatened, however, in the 1800s by an insensitive plan to build a huge brick railway bridge directly across them, linking a line from Skipton to that on the north side of the valley. It was met with disbelief and outrage, not just locally but nationally, and famous artists, writers and prominent people formed a defence association. Turner's painting of Aysgarth Falls was exhibited in a London gallery and the proposal was even brought to the notice of the House of Lords. Fortunately it was abandoned.

A mill near Yore Bridge (Yore, incidentally, is an old name for Ure) once spun yarns that were used in the manufacture of red jerseys for Garibaldi's army and for balaclavas for soldiers in the Crimean War. It now houses the Yorkshire Museum of Carriages and Horse-drawn Vehicles, with a teashop and information centre.

The churchyard of St Andrew's, overlooking the Upper Falls, is reached by 45 steps. The church contains a magnificent 15th century screen, and two bench-ends with carvings of a lion, a man with an antelope, and a rebus of William de Heslington, Abbot of Jervaulx, comprising a hazel tree, a tun and a letter W. The pieces are assumed to have come from Jervaulx Abbey.

BAINBRIDGE   Grid ref. SD 935905

The River Bain, said to be the shortest 'named' river in England, drains out of Semerwater, Yorkshire's largest natural lake, and two miles later joins the Ure at Bainbridge, the village to which it gives its name. Semerwater covers 100 acres and lies in a deep hollow. Under its waters lies an ancient village, whose church bells can sometimes be heard tolling from the depths – or so the local legend tells us! A traveller caught in a terrible storm was refused shelter at every house except one poor farmstead, and as he left he called down a curse on the village that all should be drowned by rushing waters, save the charitable household. Since evidence of a Bronze Age village has been found in and around the lake, perhaps the ancient folklore has some basis in fact after all. Not far from Semerwater, at Carr End, is the house where Dr Fothergill, the famous Quaker who founded Ackworth School, was born in 1712.

To the east of Bainbridge village, on Brough Hill, the Romans built their fort of *Virosidum*, which they occupied from the 1st to the 4th century. It has been extensively excavated, most recently in the 1950s and 60s. As well as the traces of the fort, a stretch of Roman road can be seen leading west from the village over Wether Fell. Bainbridge was established in the middle of the 12th century, probably as a home for foresters, when the area was covered by the Forest of Bainbridge, and an ancient custom from

The hornblower, Bainbridge.

this period still survives. A horn was blown in the evening, to guide belated travellers through the forest to the safety of the village. The forest is no more, but the horn is still blown at 9 pm, from the time of Hawes Back-end Fair at the Feast of Holy Rood (14th September) until Shrove Tuesday. For many generations the Metcalfe family has upheld the tradition and fulfilled the duty of hornblower. The African ox's horn, which hangs in the Rose and Crown inn, was presented to the village with great ceremony in 1864, replacing an older cow's horn, also displayed in the pub. It is said that the horn's mournful call can be heard from three miles away.

There were once two mills in the village. One is now a teashop; the other, the High Mill, after various uses, is today the property of a butcher. Thought to have been built in 1770, it was originally a corn mill, but in the early 20th century it was converted to produce electricity. The Bainbridge Electric

Lighting Company was formed in 1912, and Bainbridge, together with nearby Askrigg, enjoyed the benefits of electricity when many large industrial towns were still lit by gas.

Bainbridge is an attractive place, popular today with holiday-makers. The Rose and Crown, with the date 1445 carved on the façade, overlooks the large green where the ancient stocks stand and where in the summer months residents and visitors may be entertained by the music of a brass band.

BARKSTON ASH   *Grid ref. SE 495365*

On a small triangular grassy mound, where the main village street meets the A162 Tadcaster to Ferrybridge road, stands the ash tree which lends its name to the little village of Barkston Ash. Though there have been replacements from time to time over the years, as trees died or became diseased, an ash tree on this spot is part of a very old and continuing tradition. It is said to be planted at the very centre point of the County of Yorkshire. Looking at the map this does seem an unlikely legend, but it is claimed that aerial photographs prove it to be correct to within a distance of about a mile. True or not, it is a nice thought!

Beside the A162 road is an old coaching inn. The Ash Tree was built in 1769, when the road was a turnpike road used by the coaches travelling between York and London. In the village itself, Turpin Hall, an old mullion-windowed farmhouse, is reputed to have once sheltered the notorious highwayman Dick Turpin, who was executed in York in 1739 – not for highway robbery, but for horse stealing. Visitors to York can view the cell in which he was imprisoned, in the Castle Museum, and his grave in St George's churchyard. Incidentally, his romantic ride from London to York on his horse Black Bess is pure fiction – it never happened.

BEAMSLEY   *Grid ref. SE 082525*

Travellers on the Harrogate to Skipton road may or may not notice on their right, at the bottom of Beamsley Hill, an obviously old stone building with a coat of arms over the arched entrance. A farm of some antiquity, perhaps, with the archway leading to a courtyard, they may think in passing. That would be interesting enough. But should they stop, a closer look will disclose something quite unexpected and even more interesting. Beyond the building fronting the road, through the arch and at the end of a rising pathway, is an unusual circular building 30 feet in diameter. Tall chimneys and a lantern-top crown the roof, under which seven small rooms surround a small central chapel.

A stone in the archway tells their history. The almshouses and circular hospital – for that is what they were – were founded in 1595 by Margaret Russell, Countess of Cumberland, and 'more perfectly finished' in the 17th century by her daughter, Lady Anne Clifford, Countess of Pembroke, of Skipton Castle. The Clifford coat of arms has stood over the entrance for the hundreds of years that these unusual buildings sheltered the sick and the aged.

Sadly, perhaps, they no longer fulfil their intended function, having in recent years been converted into holiday lets.

BECKHOLE *Grid ref. NZ 822025*

The tiny picturesque moorland hamlet of Beckhole is well named. The immediate approach to it is precipitously steep, with a Z-bend halfway down. The beck (the Yorkshire word for a stream) runs alongside the road at the bottom of a deep, unfenced ravine and is crossed by a bridge at the bottom of the hill. Should you prefer to walk there from the village of Goathland, a mile away, the grassy lane that was once the old railway track is a pleasant and possibly safer alternative!

Beside the bridge is the little whitewashed pub called the Birch Hall Inn, with the unusual sight of a picture hanging on the wall, on the outside of the house. It depicts the view from the bridge of the beck as it runs through the wooded gorge behind the inn and was painted by the artist Algernon Newton (1880–1968) as a token of his affection for Beckhole, where he lived and worked during the Second World War. He painted the picture originally on a material that weathered badly, and so he painted a second – the present version – on metal, protected by glass. Newton was made a Royal Academician in 1943, but was an established and successful artist before going to Beckhole, having been one of the artists commissioned to produce art

Birch Hall Inn, Beckhole.

works for the great liner *Queen Mary* when she was built. His son, the noted actor Robert Newton, is well remembered and much imitated for his portrayal of Long John Silver in *Treasure Island*.

On a fine summer's evening, the air in Beckhole may resound to the clang of metal against metal, as the ancient game of horseshoe quoits is played on the green. The object of this game, rarely played elsewhere, is to throw the horseshoes so as to encircle a peg in the ground. It is a highly skilled and highly competitive game, with a long tradition in Beckhole.

BOLTON-ON-SWALE *Grid ref. SE 252994*

The Old Hall, next to the church at Bolton-on-Swale, a few miles from Richmond, was originally a medieval peel tower, built as defence against raiders from the north. Later, in the reign of Elizabeth I, it was added to and became a private dwelling. As all historic houses should, it is said to have its ghostly grey lady. Perhaps she is the mother of John and Christopher Wright, two of the conspirators in the Gunpowder Plot of 1603, who lived in a house which stood in what is part of the churchyard today. The two brothers were caught and put to death without trial for their part in the plot to blow up Parliament. After the death of her sons, their mother is thought to have moved into Old Hall.

The churchyard contains a memorial to a remarkable man, Henry Jenkins, reputed to have lived for 169 years. He earned his living for 140 years as a fisherman on the River Swale, and was still able to swim across the river at the age of 100. When asked about his earliest recollections, he told how, as a boy of 10 or 11, he had been sent to Northallerton with a load of arrows, destined eventually for the Battle of Flodden Field. He died in 1670, but the monument in the churchyard carrying the account of his life was not erected until 1743, when it was raised by public subscription. Its accuracy has been questioned, but it is difficult without contemporary records to be certain of the truth regarding his age, although in our own times we hear of claims of similar years for tribesmen in Afghanistan and peasants in Albania.

Not far from Bolton is Kiplin Hall, dating from about 1620. It was the home of George Calvert, Lord Baltimore, who fell from favour at the court of King James I and decided to settle in America. He was granted land there but died before he could complete matters. It was his son Leonard who, in 1633, took 300 people there – many of them from this area – to found Maryland, naming it after Henrietta Maria, the queen of Charles I. In 1973 a commemorative plaque was dedicated in Kiplin Hall by visiting Americans from Maryland and Baltimore.

BOROUGHBRIDGE *Grid ref. SE 397668*

In the distant past, anything that our ancestors were unable to explain the origins of, they were inclined to attribute to the Devil. In particular, they seem to have had the idea that he was much given to throwing stones! Disguised as a priest, he attended a religious ceremony at Aldborough, but was nevertheless unmasked. He fled, throwing huge stones behind him to destroy Aldborough, but his aim was poor and they did not reach their target. So says the legend explaining the three great monoliths of millstone grit – the so-called Devil's Arrows – at Boroughbridge.

Their true purpose is not really certain, though they may have had a religious significance. The stones, each about 20 feet high, are thought to have been transported to their present site from a quarry at Knaresborough, about 2700 BC. There were originally four stones, but one was removed around 1582 and is said to have been used in the construction of a bridge over the Tutt, a stream nearby. The three remaining stones lie in a line alongside the busy A1. They can be seen close to on the road from Boroughbridge to Roecliffe; two are in a field and the third is at the side of the road just before it meets the A1. Standing beside the roadside stone – the most easily accessible – one feels overawed by its great size and immense age.

Boroughbridge was once a stagecoach stop on the Great North Road, and its main street continued to carry heavy traffic north until the A1 brought relief. Until the 1980s that street was the scene, in the second week of June, of the annual Barnaby Horse Fair. Unfortunately, this colourful event for travelling folk had to be discontinued because of drunkenness and disorder.

The town still has a charming old-world air about it, with its little courtyards, old coaching inns and red-roofed houses. In the cobbled market square is a monumental fountain that was once the town's water supply, and the old butter market building, where the farmers' wives sold their wares. A white figure of Peace on a tall pedestal, rather than the more conventional figure of a soldier, is the town's war memorial. The River Ure falls over a weir at the edge of the town, by the fine old bridge built by Carr of York. Before local government reorganisation, it was the boundary between the North and West Ridings.

BOSSALL   *Grid ref. SE 715606*

——— Though only a hamlet today, Bossall, situated between York and Malton on the west bank of the River Derwent, was once a centre of religious importance and the court of King Edwin, the first Christian king. When Edwin became a Christian he moved his court to York, where he built a wooden church on the site of the present Minster. He was baptised there at Easter AD 627. He gave his palace at Bossall to the Church, and in AD 678 Bishop Boza or Boss of York took up residence there.

The first church, dedicated to St Botolph, was built here soon after Edwin's conversion, but the present church was erected by Paulinus de Bossall and his wife in 1180–85. The inhabitants of the village may have been wiped out by the Black Death in 1349 and there is nothing left to show where they once lived, apart from a few grassy humps and hillocks.

Paulinus's church, with its Norman arched doorway and square central tower, is a solid and imposing sight. Surrounded by a churchyard which was designated a Site of Special Scientific Interest in 1988, because of the number of wild flowers to be found within it, it is well worth a visit. The visitor in springtime can expect to see a profusion of snowdrops, primroses, wild daffodils, violets and cowslips, and other, less familiar plants, all of which are becoming increasingly rare in our fields and hedgerows.

Displayed inside the church is a copy of the record registering the marriage of the Rev Thomas Shepard and Miss Margaret Tutville in 1632. This ancient document shows an unexpected and interesting link with Harvard University in America. The Rev Shepard emigrated to America and together with a group of fellow Cambridge graduates founded a college in 1636, in the hamlet of New Towne, near Boston, Massachusetts. They originally named their college Cambridge, after their alma mater in England, but when, in 1638, the Rev John Harvard died, leaving left his library and half his estate to the college, they renamed it Harvard College in his honour. The college grew, broadening its previously narrow sectarian fields of study, eventually to achieve university status and its present-day importance.

BRANDSBY *Grid ref. SE 589724*

In the 18th century it was not uncommon for lords of the manor to demolish their villages lock, stock and barrel and rebuild them away from and out of sight of their mansions. The neat and peaceful little village of Brandsby, between Helmsley and York, on the wooded Howardian Hills is such a one. The houses once clustered around the hall but were rebuilt at the other end of the estate. The church, unique in the area, was also rebuilt in 1770, in an Italian style with a central cupola. It is reached by an avenue of lime trees and shaded by trees.

During three summers at the beginning of the 1800s, the artist John Sell Cotman came to stay at Brandsby Hall as the guest and protégé of the Cholmeleys. He was only 21 years of age at the time of his first visit, and such was the effect and influence the area had on his art that he painted some of his best works here. His well-known watercolour *The Drop Gate* was painted in Duncombe Park, the seat of the Earl of Feversham at Helmsley. He is known to have enjoyed a picnic with his patrons on the great grass terrace of Duncombe Park with its little Greek temples (see page 71) and the spectacular view of the River Rye and Rievaulx Abbey in the valley below. At Brandsby Hall his nickname – Cottey – was carved on a hornbeam, though whether by him is not known.

BRIMHAM ROCKS *Grid ref. SE 215645*

▬▬▬ Where can one see a menagerie of fantastic animals of all kinds on a hilltop in Nidderdale? If you head for Summerbridge on the B6165, some four miles from Pateley Bridge, and then take the road up the steep hillside to the north of the village, it is possible to see an elephant, a dancing bear, a hippo, tiger, rabbit, tortoise, frog – and who knows what else? – provided that your imagination is good, for these are just some of the names that have been given to the rocks on Brimham Moor.

There, 1,000 feet above sea level, are unique outcrops of millstone grit covering 60 acres. Sculpted by wind and rain over thousands of years into strange shapes, huge stones, some of them weighing hundreds of tons, rest on narrow stems or are actually rocking stones. The stone known as the Idol Rock weighs 200 tons and rests on a slender stalk only 12 inches in diameter. To wander amongst these weird and dramatic rocks, high on the moors, with panoramic views all round, is a rewarding experience. Visitors in July and August will find bilberries ripening there, the succulent ingredient of a Yorkshire delicacy known as mucky mouth pie that stains the mouth with their purple juices!

Brimham, now the property of the National Trust, once belonged to the monks of Fountains Abbey, the gift in 1280 of Roger de Mowbray, together with all the 'wild beasts and birds' of the Forest of Brimham – presumably including the ones made of stone. One wonders what they thought of them.

Brimham Rocks.

🦋 BROMPTON BY SAWDON *Grid ref. SE 945825*

There are several Bromptons in North Yorkshire. This one, about midway on the road between Pickering and Scarborough, is in the valley of the River Derwent, with the North York Moors rising on one side and the Yorkshire Wolds on the other.

The chestnut trees on the village green were planted there to commemorate the jubilee of Queen Victoria, but the name of the green, the Butts, goes back to medieval times, when archery was not just a sport but an essential skill, and this would have been the practice area. Today it is a place of pleasure and play, where picnics are a popular activity.

Although there is no longer a Cayley at Brompton Hall, it is a name that has been inseparably linked to the village since Stuart times. Perhaps its best-known bearer was Sir George Cayley (1773–1857), who has been called the father of aviation. He designed and built flying machines, experimenting with manned flight with the aid of his coachman as guinea pig, a role with which the coachman was far from happy! He is said to have given notice in 1853 immediately after his flight in what was almost

William Wordsworth was married at Brompton.

certainly the world's first glider, declaring that he had been hired to drive, not to fly. Sir George left notebooks full of ideas and details of his work to inspire future inventors, and his designs and discoveries are preserved in the library of the Aeronautical Society in Hamilton Place, London.

The 13th and 15th century church, with its square tower and tall broach spire, stands in an elevated position to the rear of the village, overlooking a small lake. It was described by Dorothy Wordsworth as a 'sweet church and churchyard', and it was here that her brother, the poet William Wordsworth, was married on October 8th 1802 to Mary Hutchinson from nearby Gallows Hill Farm. Only three of Mary's brothers and two sisters were present. Her older relatives and guardian, regarding William as a 'vagabond', disapproved of the match and had cut her off.

Despite this inauspicious start, William and Mary had a long and happy married life, although it has been suggested that William only really fell in love with Mary after ten years of marriage. A copy of their marriage certificate can be seen in the church.

BURNSALL   *Grid ref. SE 029615*

────── Burnsall, on a bend of the River Wharfe, presents the perfect picture – a gift to the artist with its old five-arched stone bridge, the church framed in trees behind, and the hills and fells forming a backdrop to the whole. The grassy banks of the broad river are popular with picnickers visiting this lovely village, and the bridge, regarded as a typical Dales bridge, is perhaps the village's most famous feature. It was donated in 1612 by Sir William Craven, who was born in the nearby village of Appletreewick.

Like Dick Whittington he left for London with scarcely a penny, made his fortune and eventually became Lord Mayor of London. He returned to his native dale to share his wealth, and in 1602 he founded the village grammar school, where the local farmers' sons were taught English and Latin free of charge, but arithmetic cost one shilling a week. In the same year he also restored Burnsall church. Notice the unusual lychgate at the church, which is closed automatically by a heavy stone weight.

Every August, Burnsall holds its sports day, when the classic fell race is run from its starting point at the famous bridge up to the summit of Burnsall Fell and down again, the contestants striving not just to be first but to create a new record time.

Not far away on the moors to the north-east is Trollers Ghyll, the wild limestone gorge said to be the haunt of Scandinavian trolls and the great spectral hound known as the Barguest, sight of which foretells death. Even today the gorge can feel very eerie and the wind play tricks with the imagination.

BUTTERTUBS PASS *Grid ref. SD 877971*

▬ The long road of Buttertubs Pass linking Upper Wensleydale with Swaledale, rises in dog-legs over the fells, with steep inclines of one in four. The 'tubs' are just beyond the top of the pass, some two miles from the village of Thwaite, and lie close to the edge and at both sides of this bleak but spectacular 1,726 feet high mountain road. They are pits in the limestone rock, caused by the effect of water and frost on existing fissures. With almost perpendicular sides, they vary in depth from shallow to 100 feet – or as some would have it 'bottomless'. In them ferns and in some cases even small trees have found shelter and flourish.

The name has been said to derive from their similarity to old-fashioned buttertubs. But tradition says that they served as a kind of primitive refrigerator for the local farmers' wives who made butter and took it to Hawes market to sell. Any that was unsold they lowered in baskets into the cool depths of the 'buttertubs' to preserve it until it could be hauled up again on the next journey to market. It may sound an unlikely story, but who can doubt the ingenuity of the past? Whether true or not, the Buttertubs are a remarkable and interesting phenomenon not to be missed.

BYLAND ABBEY *Grid ref. SE 550786*

▬ Viewed from the roadway – perhaps from beside the chained stone dogs on each side of the doorway of the Abbey Inn – the ruins of Byland Abbey, though beautiful and picturesque, give no indication of the extent of the remains. The remaining lower half of the great rose window, 26 feet in diameter, in the west front of the abbey church makes an impressive silhouette against the sky, but it is only on entering the site – now in the care of English Heritage – that one is able to appreciate that it was at one time the largest abbey of the Cistercian Order. Among the velvety green lawns, the ground plan is remarkably complete and shows the abbey to have been larger than either Fountains or nearby Rievaulx.

In 1177 monks from Furness Abbey in Lancashire, after searching for 43 years for a suitable site for a new abbey, finally settled on Byland, where they were given land by Roger de Mowbray. Before that they had had seven moves, including a period at Old Byland and at Stocking (now Oldstead). When they were at Old Byland, just two miles from Rievaulx, the bells of one house could be plainly heard in the other, to the confusion of both, and a move became necessary. The final move to the village of Wass, under the wooded Hambleton Hills, came about, when, after 30 years, the community had grown too large for the site at Stocking.

The magnificent church measuring 330 feet long, and 140 feet wide at the transepts, was repaved in the 13th century with green and yellow glazed tiles in intricate geometrical patterns, forming what was the earliest tiled floor of such a scale in the country. These beautiful medieval tiles have survived the centuries in sufficient number for us to be able to get an idea of the overall effect. They are to be seen in the transepts and presbytery, and it is wonderful that we can see them, not in a museum (though there are more in the small museum on the site), but where they were originally laid. It is difficult to realise how very old they are; they look so modern and would grace any 'executive home'.

The abbey became the centre of activity in the area. Not only did the monks have the enormous task of building the abbey itself, but also on their arrival they set to work clearing and draining the swampy ground, providing good arable land, and developing the wool trade with their large flocks of sheep. The Dissolution of the Monasteries in 1538 meant the end of Byland Abbey, but the legacy of the monks' work is still to be seen in the countryside.

CARLTON-IN-CLEVELAND   Grid ref. NZ 505045

——— Three miles south-west of Stokesley, off the A172, the unspoilt village of Carlton-in-Cleveland lies at the foot of Carlton

Bank and the Cleveland Hills. Alum Beck runs alongside the road, with the houses raised on a bank above. Near one end of the village is St Botolph's church, at the other the Methodist chapel, and in the middle that once common but now rare feature of village life, the blacksmith's shop. The 'big house' in the heart of the village dates from 1707 and it was built by the owner of the local alum works, John Prissick.

In 1894 a young Welsh priest arrived in Carlton-in-Cleveland after it had been 13 years without either church or vicar. The previous church had been mysteriously burned down and the vicar accused – but acquitted – of arson, leaving the parish demoralised and split by internal feuding. Within three years of his arrival, John Latimer Kyle had united the parishioners to raise the funds and have a new church built. He built the village school, and at his own expense a reading and recreation room for the villagers. He instituted and ran a Youth Club, one of the first to be opened in the country, in the stables of the village pub.

Amid great controversy, he bought and managed the Fox and Hounds public house (now a private house) next to the vicarage. He did not allow it to open on Sundays, but he maintained that a well-run public house fulfilled a beneficial social function for the community and decreed that all customers were to be equally welcome, including those wanting only a bottle of lemonade, a cup of tea or a meal. Inns, he said, should be more than mere drinking houses and were best run by those who were not seeking only profit.

He ran three farms, rode to hounds and went out with the guns. He loved the land and understood and appreciated those who worked on it. His own men were all allowed a day off every week, at a time when such an idea was unheard of. He was able to reach out to the villagers in a way that earned him not only their respect but their affection too. He spoke to them in their own language, on one occasion bluntly telling a farmer who asked him to pray for rain that what his land needed was not so much rain as 'a good load of muck'.

Canon Kyle, as he later became, was no ordinary village parson; many of his ideas that were ahead of time have since become commonplace. When he died in 1943, at the age of 87, he had become a Yorkshireman by adoption and a legend in his lifetime. On a personal level, I remember as a child in the thirties the buzz of excitement when he was coming to preach at our village church.

CASTLE BOLTON *Grid ref. SE 035919*

This little Wensleydale village, standing high on the hillside above the River Ure and overlooking the dale for miles around, is overshadowed by the dominating bulk of Bolton Castle – especially so in the case of the church of St Oswald, which is just a few yards from the castle.

Built in the 14th century by Richard, Lord Scrope, Chancellor of England, the castle took 18 years to complete. At 185 feet long and 130 feet wide, with huge corner towers 100 feet high, this grey and forbidding fortress is one of the most impressive and remarkable in the country. It is open to the public daily.

It was besieged by Cromwell in the Civil War and much of it is ruined, but there remains a great deal of interest to be seen: the armoury, the stables, the kitchen, various rooms with period tableaux, and the dark dank oubliette – its only opening a hole in the ceiling – where once an arm bone attached to an iron ring was found. It is hard to imagine the cruelty that could condemn someone to rot down there. An interesting detail in the ruined well room is the remains of a shaft that allowed water to be drawn directly from the well to the rooms above.

In the summer of 1568 Mary, Queen of Scots became a prisoner in the castle. Though the six months that she spent there were passed in comparative comfort, attended by a retinue of forty servants and engaged in pursuits such as riding, writing and needlework, she plotted constantly and managed to escape. However, she was recaptured in nearby Leyburn, and found herself exchanging the castle for a more secure prison further south.

A young artist, Fred Lawson (1888–1968), visited Castle Bolton on a day trip in 1910, fell in love with the area and resolved to live there. He settled in the village the following year and spent the rest of his life drawing and painting the scenery and life of Wensleydale. He and his artist wife, Muriel, gathered around them artists and writers – the Bolton Group – who through their work made the dale more widely known.

CATTERICK *Grid ref. SE 241980*

—— Once the Roman eagle was raised here, where now the Union Jack flies; at the time of the Romans it was a military camp, as it is today. The name of Catterick is synonymous with Britain's largest military base, a garrison of 7,500 regular soldiers occupying a site of 2,400 acres situated four miles from the actual town. The additional extensive training grounds include large areas of lovely countryside, much of it designated a Site of Special Scientific Interest. Once Roman chariots and soldiers may have passed through Catterick along the road from York to Hadrian's Wall. Certainly stage coaches and later motor traffic on the Great North Road clattered and thundered through the town and over the 15th century bridge across the Swale, until the road was diverted.

The monk Paulinus, later to become Archbishop of York, was sent from Rome in the 7th century to aid Augustine in the conversion of the people to Christianity. He baptised so many thousands in the River Swale at Catterick that the river became known as the Jordan of England and the Holy River. Windows in the church, built about 1415 by Catherine de Burgh, whose family rose from the peasantry to wealthy landowners, show Paulinus and the baptisms, and also depict him preaching to King Edwin, who was one of his converts. In 1816 Dr Alexander Scott came to the church at Catterick as its vicar. He had been on board the *Victory* at Trafalgar, and it was to him that Nelson spoke his dying words, pleading that Lady Hamilton and his daughter Horatia should not be forgotten, before breathing his last with the words, 'God and my country.' Scott lived in the town until his death in 1840.

Catterick is well known to the followers of the sport of horseracing and people flock to the race meetings there. The racecourse is also home to another popular activity. It holds the largest Sunday market in the North of England, a colourful sight stretching as far as the eye can see, with hundreds of stalls selling everything one can think of.

CAWOOD *Grid ref. SE 575375*

—— From the north, entry to the town is over the River Ouse, via what was once a toll bridge. Cawood lies at a bend in the

Ouse, close to the point where it is joined by the Wharfe, so it is no surprise to learn that it was once important as an inland port and a centre of the boat building industry. The nautical sounding names of its public houses are a clue to that part of its past. More recently the Selby coalfield and nearby power stations have brought welcome jobs in addition to the long-standing tradition of agriculture and market gardening.

This small town has a long and splendid history. It was known as the Windsor of the North when Cawood Castle was visited by royalty in medieval times. In the 14th century it became the palace of the Archbishops of York and saw scenes of unbelievable opulence and feasting that lasted for days at a time. We are told that George Neville in 1456 celebrated his elevation to archbishop with the aid of 1,000 cooks, who prepared a feast for his many guests of 100 oxen, 1,000 sheep, 2,000 pigs, 500 deer, 4,000 rabbits, 4,000 ducks, 2,000 chickens, 2,000 geese, 4,000

Cawood Castle.

pigeons and 600 pike and bream – and these were just some of the ingredients. They quenched their thirst with 300 tuns of ale and 100 tuns of wine.

All that remains of the palace today is the gatehouse and the 15th century building known as the Banqueting Hall, now referred to as Cawood Castle. Perhaps the most famous of the castle's occupants was Cardinal Wolsey, who came in 1530, but was arrested here for high treason and died at Leicester on his way to trial in London. There is a story that he was hidden by the townspeople, by whom he was well loved, in the cellars of the Ferry Inn, but if so their efforts were in vain. Children chanting the nursery rhyme about the sad fate of Humpty Dumpty cannot know that it refers, not to the egg depicted in their picture books, but to Thomas Wolsey, who had a great fall and could not be put together again.

In the church, which stands on the bank of the Ouse not far from the castle, is a memorial to George Mountain, the son of a poor farmer, who became Bishop of Durham. When asked by King Charles whom he should appoint as Archbishop of York, he is reputed to have put forward his own cause, with the words, 'Thou shouldst say to this Mountain, "Be removed and cast into the See".' He achieved his ambition, but sadly not for long; he died in the night on the day of his enthronement.

CHOP GATE *Grid ref. SE 555995*

Almost half of the North York Moors National Park is heather-clad moorland, the largest area of heather-covered upland in England. It is divided by river valleys or dales; Bilsdale, Farndale and Rosedale are three dales running almost parallel to each other through the moors, and of these Bilsdale is the widest, an area of scattered farms and hamlets. Chop Gate (pronounced *yat* in the local dialect) is Bilsdale's only village. The River Seph and the B1257 Helmsley to Stokesley road run through the dale, giving wonderful views and walking opportunities, and the Cleveland Way passes close by. There is a great sporting and hunting tradition in the dale, Bilsdale Foxhounds being one of the oldest packs in the country.

One of the oldest buildings in the National Park, Spout House, stands at the roadside not far from Chop Gate. It is a long low thatched house of cruck construction, dating from 1550. It took its name from a spring in the hillside behind it, and, though renamed the Sun Inn when it was granted a licence in 1714, the old name stuck. Today it is possible for visitors to see its traditionally furnished interior, from Easter to October, between 10 am and 4 pm on any day except Thursday.

At the new Sun Inn close by, an unusual reminder of a former sporting patron can be seen at any time.

Bobby Dowson was wicket keeper for Spout House cricket club, and served as whipper-in for the Bilsdale Hunt for over 60 years. He died in 1902 and at his funeral his coffin was accompanied by horses and hounds. His hunting clothes were buried with him, but his gravestone, carved with a fox's head and hunting whips, was deemed by the vicar unsuitable for inclusion in consecrated ground.

It lay outside the gate of the churchyard for 12 years. Then, when the new Sun Inn was built next to the old Spout House, Bobby's sporting friends decided that because of his fondness for the old pub the new inn would be an appropriate site for his memorial. And so the cross with its hunting symbols was placed by the entrance to the Sun Inn, where it still stands.

A small plain cross marks the grave of Bobby Dowson in Urra churchyard at the head of the dale, with the words,

'No finer sportsman ever followed hounds
O'er moors and fields he knew for thirty miles around.'

CLAPHAM *Grid ref. SD 745695*

—— A veritable Mecca for tourists, Clapham is in the south-west corner of the Yorkshire Dales National Park. This jewel of a village is the base for the most popular route for the ascent of Ingleborough (2,372 feet), on whose flank it is situated. It is also the home of the famous Ingleborough Cave, with its underground wonderland of stalactites and stalagmites, that first opened to the public in 1837. Clapham Beck, which rises on Ingleborough, cuts through the village, dividing it into two parts joined by stone bridges. Halfway down the hill, the stream flows into the enormous depths of Gaping Ghyll, a vast cavern capable of swallowing St Paul's Cathedral with room to spare! At certain times of the year, members of the public brave enough to make the descent can experience the thrill of being winched to the bottom in a kind of bosun's chair, by the Cave Rescue Association.

As you walk through the village, note how many of the old houses have pigeon-holes in their gables. Pigeon meat in days gone by was an important source of food – and pigeon pie a popular dish. Ingleborough Hall, now an outdoor centre, is the largest building in the village. It was once the home of the Farrers, a family of explorers and scientists. Most famous was Reginald Farrer, after whom many species of flowers are named. He travelled the world gathering plants and died in Burma in 1920 on one of his flower hunting expeditions, aged only 40. It is said that he would make straight for his potting shed on returning from his journeys, to make sure that his precious new plants were properly cared for, before even entering his home. The mile-long trail to Ingleborough Cavern passes through the estate and the landscape that this dedicated botanist helped to create. A memorial column to his memory stands in the village.

Clapham's other famous son is Michael Faraday, the physicist and assistant to Sir Humphrey Davy, who has been called the father of electricity. He was born here in the village, the son of the blacksmith.

It was here too that Harry Scott founded and produced from his own home the popular Yorkshire magazine *The Dalesman*, now grown and expanded and based in Skipton.

COXWOLD *Grid ref. SE 535775*

—— The 18th century author Laurence Sterne spent the last eight years of his life in this picturesque village. It was here that he wrote *The Life and Opinions of Tristram Shandy* and *A Sentimental Journey* while earning his living as a country parson. He was, however, described at the time as 'not the kind of priest in whom the Anglican Church can feel proud'.

Coxwold in the 21st century still has an air of old world charm, with its pretty cottages and dignified houses, and the almshouses, endowed in 1662 by Mary, the daughter of Oliver Cromwell, who became Lady Fauconberg and mistress of nearby Newburgh Priory. The wide village street with its grassy banks and cobbled areas rises up to the church, which has an unusual octagonal tower. Opposite the church is a gabled house with huge buttressed chimneys, one of which has the odd architectural feature of a window in it.

This is Shandy Hall, where Sterne lived, which is named after the character in his book, but dates back to medieval times. Originally a timber-framed open hall dwelling, it was always a priest's house, as was confirmed by a medieval wall painting from about 1450, depicting religious subjects, which was discovered hidden behind panelling during restoration in the late 1960s. The house has been open to the public on selected days during the summer months since 1973, restored essentially to the state in which Sterne left it.

Sterne's remains lie beside the church where he served so happily. He died in London on a visit in 1768 and was interred in the burial ground of St George's church in Hanover Square. When that ground was cleared for development in 1969, his remains were brought to Coxwold for reburial. There is a story, which may or may not be true, that his body was taken by bodysnatchers, but on being recognised on the dissection table was hastily returned. Not one but two gravestones commemorate him at Coxwold, and

Shandy Hall, Coxwold.

those who study them carefully will be puzzled to notice that one gives his date of death as September 13th 1768, while the other has the correct date of March 18th 1768. One wonders how such a significant mistake could have been made.

In the church, the chancel has an unusual long U-shaped altar rail, necessitated by the many monuments to past members of the Belasis and Fauconberg families from Newburgh Priory that crowd it. On the Dissolution of the Monasteries, the priory was granted by Henry VIII to the Belasis family, and it became their home and that of their descendants. Sir George Wombwell, a recent ancestor, was one of the very few survivors of the Light Brigade at Balaclava. He died in 1913. Newburgh Priory stands back from the road to Crayke, about half a mile from Coxwold, fronted by elegant wrought iron gates and a roadside lake, where many motorists stop their cars to feed the swans and other waterfowl.

The Belasyes line became barons and viscounts in the 1600s, and Mary, Cromwell's daughter, became the second wife of Thomas, 1st Earl Fauconberg. When a vengeful Charles II had Cromwell's body disinterred, hung and beheaded, Lady Fauconberg is reputed to have had the headless body of her father brought to Newburgh Priory, where it is said to rest in a simple brick tomb in an attic room.

The priory, like Shandy Hall, is opened to the public and so the visitor may visit the Cromwell Room as it is known, but the tomb has never been opened and keeps its secret still. Even Edward VII, then Prince of Wales, on a visit to Sir George Wombwell at Newburgh Priory was denied his request to see inside the tomb. No one can say for certain whether the story is true but if Cromwell does indeed lie there he does so undisturbed.

CRAYKE *Grid ref. SE 562706*

——— The village of Crayke is visible from afar, rising as it does out of the Plain of York on a little hill. The houses climb up to the church and castle at the summit, from where the plain in its turn can be viewed for miles around. A seat has been thoughtfully provided at the top of the hill so that one can take in the wonderful panorama of agricultural countryside stretching out below.

The castle, built on the site of a Norman castle, dates from the 15th century and consists of two separate buildings, one of which is a private dwelling. The church, built in or around 1436, is said to stand on the spot where the body of St Cuthbert rested before it reached its final resting place in Durham Cathedral and is dedicated to him. Crayke and the area for three miles around was granted to Cuthbert in AD 658 as a place to break his journeys between York and Lindisfarne and was for centuries owned by the bishopric of Durham. It thus became a part of Durham County within the county of Yorkshire, and as such was often used by wrongdoers to evade the law by crossing from one county to the other. The name of the village pub, The Durham Ox, is a reminder of this anomalous connection.

Below the church is a cottage bearing a plaque proclaiming it to be the birthplace in 1860 of the controversial Dean Inge of St Paul's Cathedral. He describes in his writings the strict religious observance with which he was brought up in a clerical family, which meant that few pleasures were allowed on Sundays. A work on the Christian martyrs, describing in detail the ingenious tortures to which they were subjected, was, he said, 'the only amusing book we were allowed to read on Sunday'. He also tells of an incident when the portable barrel organ used in the church interrupted the service by sticking and continuing to play despite all efforts to stop it, so that eventually it had to be carried out into the churchyard. One can imagine the dismay of the older members of the congregation and the stifled giggling of the young ones at this amusing event.

William Ralph Inge was an original thinker, who had a brilliant career, and despite his unorthodox views – often regarded as too pessimistic – about society then and in the future, Crayke is proud to claim him as its most famous son.

CROFT-ON-TEES *Grid ref. NZ 295095*

—— Mention the Tees to most people and there will immediately spring to mind an unattractive industrial landscape, although from its source along most of its length the river runs through pleasant countryside. Croft, once a small spa town famous for its wells, is certainly on the River Tees, but with no suggestion of the industry to be found a dozen miles away at the mouth of the river. So close to the county boundary does it lie that 95 yards of the seven-arched bridge crossing the river here are in Yorkshire and 53 yards are in County Durham. A blue stone on the third arch from the Durham side marks the boundary line.

Little evidence of its past as a spa remains, except for the very fine Croft Spa Hotel, which was built to accommodate the visitors who came for treatment. The waters, taken both internally and externally, were reputedly particularly effective for diseases of the skin.

Not far from the hotel is St Peter's church and within it is what must surely be one of the most grandiose family pews in the country. Installed during the Restoration period (1660s or 1670s), it is a strong reminder of the rigid class distinctions in society at the time. The Millbanke family from Hanlaby Hall (now demolished), three miles away, ascended by an imposing balustraded stairway of three small flights to their spacious curtained chamber, elevated well above the parson in his pulpit and quite removed from the common people below. It has been described as a little wooden house on stilts. Lord Byron, who married one of the Millbanke daughters, probably sat here with his new bride during his unhappy honeymoon at Hanlaby Hall. George Hudson, the railway king, and his wife also sat here in elevated style, though they appear to have wished to be to some extent unobserved. George is said to have stood always with his back to the parson when he sang, and Mrs Hudson hid delicately behind her parasol during the sermon!

By the main door in the church is a large carving 2 feet high and $1^{1}/_{2}$ feet wide, of a kind which one might be surprised to find in a religious setting. Known as a Sheela Na Gig, it is a crudely carved figure of a squatting female, her legs splayed to expose her genitalia. Such figures are found in Norman churches, usually placed near a door, but are generally accepted as being Celtic in origin.

In the sanctuary, another carved stone, of a grinning cat, was almost certainly the inspiration for the Cheshire Cat in *Alice in Wonderland*. Charles Lutwidge Dodgson, later known as Lewis Carroll, came to Croft in 1843, at the age of 11, when his father became rector here, and would have known the church well. In the garden of the rectory opposite the church Charles built a miniature railway, complete in all its details, with signals, stations and tickets, to amuse his younger siblings and indulge his own passionate interest in everything to do with railways.

Not everyone had the same delight in railways, however; when the railway came to the area, the Chaytors of Croft Hall completely changed the orientation of the hall so as not to be able to see it.

Like so many other places in Yorkshire, during the Second World War Croft learned to live with the proximity of an airfield and the drone of heavy bombers taking off on their raids. Today the sounds of engines are still to be heard on its runways, for it is now a motor racing circuit. But the bomber crews are not forgotten; a memorial to them stands at the junction of the road out of nearby Dalton.

CROPTON *Grid ref. SE 755895*

Situated on the edge of the moors, Cropton has one very broad street of stone houses with red pantiled roofs; they were once cruck houses and longhouses, but only two still retain their medieval crucks. This is a typical village of the area.

Outside the church is the stump of an ancient cross on which there used to be placed a cup filled with water for the refreshment of travellers, a practice remembered in the rhyme, 'On Cropton cross there is a cup, and in the cup there is a sup.' The present-day traveller can 'sup' to quench his thirst at the New Inn, which brews its own beers, popular with fans of real ale. Indeed, the enthusiast might visit the inn and the village for a beer-tasting weekend – a beer festival in miniature, as it were!

For centuries Cropton was a place where limestone was quarried and burnt in kilns, the end product being carted throughout a wide area for use on the land. This one-time industry accounts for the hollows still to be seen to the south of the village.

Today many visitors are drawn to the village by the remains of the Cawthorne Roman training camps lying between here and nearby Newton. There are four, covering about 25 acres. The oldest is said to date from the time of Agricola; the other three were probably built about the same time as Hadrian was building his wall further north.

The mound in the village, where once a Norman castle stood, now makes an excellent viewpoint for the visitor to scan the surrounding countryside – not for enemies, but for that perfect shot of the splendid landscape.

DALBY *Grid ref. SE 635715*

Treading the maze was once a regular entertainment in both town and country life, though the rules and origins of the ancient game have long been lost. Shakespeare makes mention of it in *A Midsummer Night's Dream*, when Titania complains to Oberon, 'The nine men's morris is filled up with mud, And the quaint mazes in the wanton green, For lack of tread are indistinguishable.' The only surviving example of such a maze in North Yorkshire is well kept and clearly distinguishable, cut into the turf beside the quiet country byroad leading from the village of Terrington to Dalby and, rather oddly, some distance from any habitation.

Various names are given to the mazes in different parts of the country: Julian's Bower, Robin Hood's Race, Shepherd's Ring, Mismaze, Walls of Troy, Troy Town, or, as this particular example has always been known, City of Troy. In some cathedrals and churches in France, and occasionally in England, a maze was used as a symbol of life with its many difficulties and trials, leading eventually to Jerusalem, the name given to the centre of the maze, and the ultimate goal of the virtuous. It may be seen as a pattern on the floor or elsewhere in the church, such as a roof boss, and it is interesting to speculate which came first. Was the game taken as a symbol by the church, or did the game evolve from the church's symbolism?

Standing beside the Dalby maze, it is difficult to imagine just what the game entailed. With a turf maze such as this – unlike one with hedges – one can see clearly where one is going, and it is intriguing to consider what the rules might have been that made it more interesting than simply walking through it.

DANBY *Grid ref. NZ 705085*

When Canon John Atkinson (1814–1900) was going to the remote parish of Danby, a friend declared: 'Danby was not found out when they sent Bonaparte to St Helena, or else they never would have taken the trouble to send him all the way there!' Canon Atkinson nevertheless remained in Danby for 53 years and grew to know and love the moors and dales and the people in them. It was there that he wrote *Forty Years in a Moorland Parish*, which chronicles the antiquities of the area and the customs and superstitions of its people.

Amongst those superstitions, witchposts may have been considered a necessary device to protect a household from the evil influences of witchcraft. An example of a witchpost can be seen in a cruck cottage from Stang End at Danby, now reconstructed in the museum at Hutton-le-Hole (see page 79). Other examples are to be found in Pannet Park Museum in Whitby, where the Danby hand-of-glory is also on display. This grisly object, found in a cottage at Danby, was once used as a charm by burglars. A human hand severed from the body of a criminal still hanging on the gallows was dried, pickled and cured, and then used as a holder for a candle gruesomely made from the fat of a hanged man, in the belief that when carried on a burglary it would make the criminal invisible. Sleeping people would remain asleep and those who were awake remain awake, making it a highly desirable charm therefore for those who conducted their villainies at night. The charm could only be broken by extinguishing the flame, and this could only be achieved by pouring over it either milk or blood. Since, until 1837, the penalty for burglary was death, it is not surprising that criminals clutched at any chance to avoid capture, even putting their faith in such bizarre charms. When the penalty was reduced to imprisonment the hand-of-glory gradually fell into disuse. The Danby hand is thought to have last been used in 1820.

In the early 1300s, the Latimers, one of the powerful families who owned large parts of Yorkshire, built Danby Castle on the end of the ridge between Danby Dale and Little Fryup Dale. Katherine Parr, Henry VIII's widow, lived there for some years with her second husband John Latimer. A considerable portion of the castle remains and is incorporated into a farmhouse. A medieval bridge crossing the River Esk below Danby Castle is known as Duck Bridge, taking its name from George Duck, a local stonemason who restored it in the early 18th century, but it originates from the same period as the castle, and is regarded by many as the most perfect example of its kind.

Danby is no longer the remote place of Canon Atkinson's time, but the very hub of the North York Moors National Park. Danby Lodge, once a shooting lodge, is now the visitors' centre, where exhibitions, activities and a wealth of information on all aspects of the national park are to be found.

DRAX *Grid ref. SE 675265*

Drax in Norman times had a castle, a priory and a church. Philip de Tolleville held his heavily fortified castle there and stood against Stephen, but in 1154 Henry II, in one of the first acts of his reign to make an impact on Yorkshire, took the castle by storm and destroyed it. Officially, it was necessary to obtain royal permission to build a castle, but many barons acted without permission and built what were called adulterine castles. In so doing they risked the king's order of destruction, or of being turned out and dispossessed. Nothing now remains of de Tolleville's castle except a wooded mound and the name Castle Hill Farm to remind anyone that it was ever there. Just a few stones remain of the priory, which has vanished too, but once stood by the River Ouse. Only the church stands as a reminder of the village's Norman past.

Drax and the neighbouring village of Camblesforth are overshadowed by Drax power station with its many cooling towers and 860 feet high chimney. The largest coal-fired power station in Europe, it generates one tenth of Britain's total electricity demand. Larger than any Norman castle, though perhaps not as aesthetically pleasing, it has brought employment and expansion to the two villages, including a huge 30 acre greenhouse complex, heated by steam from the power station. Interested visitors can take guided tours of the station, and it has to be said that not everyone finds the industrial landscape unpleasant. Lesley Garrett, the internationally famed opera singer who spent her childhood in the vicinity of Drax, is on record as saying that she finds power stations an attractive and comforting sight. Certainly the sunset behind Drax's towers makes a beautifully dramatic picture.

In 1667, Charles Read, a wealthy shipper born in Drax, founded the ancient grammar school there, which bears his name. He also established schools in Tuxford and Corby, making it a rule that the pupils of all the schools should take turns to sweep out the schoolhouse every Saturday afternoon, or pay the penalty of a sixpenny fine. Whether the old rule still applies I do not know. Perhaps today they use a vacuum cleaner – a useful accomplishment for life after school!

EASINGWOLD *Grid ref. SE 535695*

Easingwold once stood in the ancient Forest of Galtres and the courts to try those who broke the laws of the forest were held there. Later in its history it became an important staging post for the Royal Mail between York and Edinburgh, and later still heavy goods traffic thundered along Long Street, part of the A19, on its way to and from the north. Today a bypass has relieved this pleasant market town, with its shops, pubs and Georgian houses enclosing a cobbled market square. In the centre of the square, where the weekly market is held on Friday, is the old town hall, which over the years has been the fire station, the cinema and a printing works.

Easingwold was once linked to the main railway line to Edinburgh by a branch line to Alne, opened in 1891. Its earliest engine was known affectionately as The Coffee Pot because of its shape and was in use up to 1948. The engine driver knew most of his passengers and on occasion was known to have backed up his train to pick up tardy children travelling to and from the grammar school. The old grammar school is now a primary school since a modern comprehensive was built on the southern edge of the town.

The parish church, dedicated to St John the Baptist and All Saints, stands prominently on a rise at the northern end of the town and is well worth a visit. The interior is colourful, with medieval greens and reds on the chancel ceiling and the gallery. A sombre note is added by the narrow black parish coffin, made between 1645 and 1646, and one of only two in the country. Those parishioners who were too poor to afford to pay for their burial were carried to their grave in this stark unpolished coffin of rough common wood.

A stone in the north wall of the sanctuary comes from the church of Samaria where it is said the head of John the Baptist was discovered. Outside the church, by the chancel door, is the grave of Ann Harrison, known as Nanna Ran Dan. She once kept an inn, now demolished, in the area of Easingwold named Uppleby. Legend has it that Nanna will rise from her grave if at midnight one runs round it three times and spits upon it. I do not know if anyone has ever put it to the test! The inscription on her gravestone suggests that she would be an interesting person to meet, were it possible. Though difficult to read because of age and lichens, it describes Ann, who died, aged 80, in 1715:

'Chaste but no Prude and though Free yet no Harlot
By Principle Virtuous by Education a Protestant
Her Freedom made her liable to Censure
Whilst her extensive Charity made her esteemed
Her tongue and her hands were ungovernable
But the rest of her members she kept in Subjection.'

We are finally exhorted to 'Be Charitable and speak well of her'.

EAST HARLSEY *Grid ref. SE 425995*

—— East Harlsey lies 5 miles north-east of Northallerton, looking out over a landscape of the Hambleton Hills to the south and the spectacular views of the Cleveland Hills to the east. At one end of the long village street of houses old and new and the pub with the unusual name of the Cat and Bagpipes, an avenue of grand old trees leads to the hall. Beside it a lane takes one down to the little church, in a delightful setting above a deep glen. Close to the boundary of the churchyard stands a square brick building with a pyramidal roof, resembling a defensive tower, but the small openings in its sides indicate its true purpose. It is a dovecot dating from the late 17th century.

To own a dovecot was originally the prerogative of the lord of the manor, not as a decorative feature of his domain, but for the purely practical purpose of providing food – along with his stew (fishpond), his rabbit warren and his park full of deer. Ancient dovecots are usually to be found by the manor house, the church or the manor farm, and the one at East Harlsey is indeed on a farm, close by both church and big house. It is thought to be one of the earliest buildings on the East Harlsey estate, but as time progressed it would, like many others, have become redundant, and has over the years been given various uses. In 1908 it was converted to use as a water tank and has also been used more recently as a stable. Today an even more imaginative use has been found for this Grade II listed building. In the year 2000 it was offered by the Rural Buildings Trust, at a payment of only £1 per annum, with planning permission granted for its conversion to a tiny one-bedroom 'character residence', subject to there being no change to the architectural features of its outward appearance.

It is certainly unique and possibly the house with the smallest windows in the country – and the largest electricity bill!

EBBERSTON   *Grid ref. SE 895825*

Ebberston is in the Vale of Pickering, situated about 5 miles from Pickering on the road to Scarborough. Opposite the parish church of St Mary, which is at some distance from the village itself, is a field known as the Bloody Field, where in AD 704 King Alchfrid of Northumbria fought a battle with his father King Oswy. The stream through the field was said to run red with the blood of the dead warriors, and is referred to as the Bloody Beck. High in the wood (an area belonging to the Yorkshire Wildlife Trust) to the north of the village is a cairn marking Alfred's Cave, where Alchfrid (or Alfred) is reputed to have rested after being wounded in the battle. He was taken from there to Little Driffield, where he died and is buried.

Close to the church is the tiny Palladian mansion that is Ebberston Hall. It has been described as the smallest stately home in England, and was built in 1718 for William Thompson, Member of Parliament for Scarborough and Master of the Mint for Queen Anne. It is one storey high and has only eleven rooms. Colen Campbell, its architect, who later became architect to the Prince of Wales, described his work as 'a Rustick Edifice'. It is supposed to have been intended to win for William Thompson the love of a certain lady, but as far as is known she never even visited there. It may well have been meant to be a hunting lodge rather than a love nest.

A century later it became the property of George Osbaldeston, the Regency eccentric who was known as the 'Sporting Squire of England' because of his interest and excellence in many sporting activities. He was born in the village of Hutton Buscel, not far away, but whilst celebrating his 21st birthday in 1808, his home, the Old Hall, caught fire and was burned down, and so George went to live at Ebberston.

He bought his first pack of hounds while an undergraduate at Oxford and hunted six days a week. His favourite hound, Vaulter, he maintained was well behaved because it had swallowed a prayer book! He left Oxford without a degree and gambled away most of his money, so that when he demolished the two small wings of Ebberston Hall, intending to build bigger ones, he could never afford to do so. In the early 1900s Sir Kenelm Cayley dismantled the cupola of the hall in order to sell the lead. Nevertheless the house is still an elegant and well-proportioned miniature of classical architecture, and the present owners strive to maintain and preserve it, opening it to the public between Easter and September.

Before leaving Ebberston, if visiting the village's only pub, look out for the 'Old Peculier' clock – which makes time go backwards!

EGTON BRIDGE *Grid ref. SE 805055*

The Roman Catholic church of St Hedda in the village of Egton Bridge honours Father Nicholas Postgate, who said Mass and conducted baptisms and other ceremonies of the Roman Catholic faith when it was forbidden by law and Roman Catholics were persecuted and died for their religion. His shrine in the church contains a crucifix, candlesticks, a missal and a priest's vestment, together with other relics from his secret chapel. The reliefs of the Stations of the Cross inside the church are an interesting feature, as are the colourful scenes from the life of Jesus, depicted on panels around the outside walls of this large and imposing building.

Father Postgate was born in Egton Bridge about 1597 and was hung, drawn and quartered on the Knavesmire in York at the age of 82, after being betrayed for baptising a child. He had been ordained in France in 1628 and served as secret chaplain to various landed families in England before returning to his native North York Moors to serve as priest to the poor, at the age of 62. Tramping the moors in all weathers, despite his age, he conducted secret services, giving notice of them by pre-arranged signals using sheets ostensibly drying on the hedgerows, a common method of drying laundry amongst country folk.

Leaving Egton Bridge on the road to Egton, look out for a cottage on the right-hand side (past the house of the Cleveland Girl Guides) with the name of Mass House. It is set back from the road on a slight rise, and so easy to miss when travelling in the opposite direction – from Egton into Egton Bridge. The original house, a low thatched building, had to be demolished in 1928 as it was considered beyond repair. In 1830, however, a wall in the old house had collapsed, revealing Father Postgate's secret chapel – a small loft, still containing an altar made ready for the Mass which was heard by his congregation in the kitchen below. A secret exit in the roof at the back of the house made escape possible for the priest if it became necessary. Note the carved name stone on the gable wall of the present building erected on the site of the old house. It indicates as nearly as possible the position of the secret chapel.

Egton Bridge has long been the venue of a curious and unusual event, held every year on the first Tuesday in August, namely its famous Gooseberry Show, at which gooseberries as big as golf balls, and even bigger, are the norm! Once such shows were popular, but of those listed in the official Register of Shows in 1857, that at Egton Bridge is the sole survivor.

FARNDALE *Grid ref. SE 665975*

—— A long narrow dale in the moors north of Kirkbymoorside, Farndale is famed for its wild daffodils, stretching for 5 miles along the banks of the River Dove, and attracting crowds of visitors between March and May. These are the true wild daffodils, tiny yellow blooms known locally as Lenten lilies because of the time at which they flower, and thought to have been planted by monks in the 12th century. It has even been suggested that these were the 'host of golden daffodils' that inspired Wordsworth's poem, and certainly he was familiar with this area but it does seem unlikely. At one time put in danger of extinction by plundering visitors, the daffodils are now protected by law and wardens patrol the area, which was made a nature reserve in 1953, to ensure that no one picks the flowers.

Visitors, however, have not been the only danger to the valley. Though it is hard to believe, this beautiful dale has twice been threatened by flooding as a reservoir for the city of Hull. In 1933 Hull Corporation obtained parliamentary powers to do just that, but nothing was done until the scheme was revived in the 1960s. Vigorous opposition, petitions and lobbying of Parliament fortunately led to success in defeating the plan.

Like that other lovely valley of Rosedale, Farndale has a history of industry. Coal, ironstone, gravel and jet have all been worked here in the past, but today Farndale is a community of scattered farms and just three hamlets: Lowna, Low Mills and Church Houses. At Lowna an old burial ground is the resting place of 114 Quakers, buried there between 1675 and 1837.

Once isolated and remote, areas of the North York Moors have always been places of strange legends and folklore, full of witches and hobgoblins. Farndale is no exception, and in particular is the home of the hob. A hob will help a farmer by working unseen at tasks during the night, for no reward other than a bowl of cream. But woe betide anyone who should happen to see the hob, who always works naked, or fails to leave out his bowl of cream! All manner of tricks and mischief will result. There is a story of a Farndale farmer so pestered and plagued by a hob he had offended that he decided to move house. As he was leaving, with his goods piled up on a cart, he met a neighbour who remarked, 'I see you're flitting then.' Before the farmer could reply, a little voice from the milk churn on the back of the cart piped up, 'Aye we're flitting,' whereupon the farmer wearily decided that if the hob was going too he might as well stay where he was!

FILEY *Grid ref. TA 115805*

'It is ideal for the children.' This is what everyone immediately says about the small traditional seaside resort of Filey. And so it is, with its 5 mile stretch of sandy beach, but there is plenty there for the adults as well in the way of shops and entertainments. The Century Way from Filey to York and many good coastal walks can be enjoyed by the energetic. Its most famous feature is the remarkable geological curiosity known as Filey Brigg, an outcrop of rock to the north of the town, reaching

The Boy Bishop, Filey.

like a natural pier almost a mile out to sea. It is possible at low tide to reach the Brigg across the sands and at other times down steps from the cliff top, where the Romans once had a signal station, and to walk along it, exploring its rocks and pools. The currents are strong and the breakers can be fierce, however, and a wary eye should be kept on the weather and the tides. Anglers in the past have been swept away and ships have been wrecked on the rocks. The Brigg is said to take its name from an Old Norse word meaning 'landing place', though because of its dangers it would seem a place for ships to avoid.

The Devil – or perhaps it was the local giant Wade – decided to build a causeway from Filey all the way across the North Sea, but soon became discouraged with the task. As he was packing up his tools to leave he dropped his hammer in the water, and, thrusting his hand into the sea to retrieve it, grasped instead a fish between his thumb and finger. That is how Filey Brigg came about, and how at the same time the haddock got its distinctive markings – or so the legend would have us believe!

The church of St Oswald in Church Ravine is appropriately dedicated to the patron saint of fishermen and a window in the church, known as the Fishermen's Window, dating from 1885, remembers the local men lost at sea whose bodies were never recovered. On the wall next to the window is a memorial, a reminder of a curious old custom from a much earlier age, which was discontinued after the Reformation as sacrilegious. In medieval times, in certain church revels, a boy was chosen from the choir or grammar school in a large parish, to play the part of the Boy Bishop. From December 6th, the day of St Nicholas, patron saint of children, until Holy Innocents' Day, December 28th, the boy presided over church services, invested with the full insignia of a bishop, and was responsible for the behaviour of other boys dressed as priests. The odd little memorial in St Oswald's, which appears to commemorate a Boy Bishop who must have died in office, is dated between 1250 and 1300.

FOSTON *Grid ref. SE 693650*

—— At the foot of the Howardian Hills, not far from the grandeur of Castle Howard, is the little village of Foston, consisting of a few cottages and farms in agricultural countryside. It is pleasant but undistinguished. Its most remarkable building is the small bellcote church, not only because of its Norman doorway with its panels of figures and animals, but also because of its literary connection. It was here as rector of this little church of All Saints that the great man of letters Sydney Smith spent 22 years of his life, from 1807 to 1829. A noted wit, he had declared himself as having 'no relish for the country. It is a kind of healthy grave' and to have said, 'In the country I always fear that creation will expire before teatime.' It is not easy therefore to imagine this man of learning, advocate of social and religious reform and lecturer in moral philosophy, living in this quiet spot in the house he built himself near Thornton-le-Clay, a mile away. As a welcome guest at Castle Howard and in county society, presumably he was able to enjoy some of the finer things of life otherwise unobtainable in his humble parish. He did not neglect his parishioners, however, and worked hard for their improvement and welfare. He is

Memorial to Sydney Smith, Foston church.

remembered in the church by a handsome bronze memorial bearing his profile and an inscription praising his virtues both as rector and man.

Also inside the church are two prayer boards – a common enough feature in the 18th and early 19th centuries – but these particular boards contain a simple error in the wording. It is amusing to speculate whether Sydney Smith, so skilful with words himself, ever read them and if so what his reaction would have been. A kindly man, he no doubt excused the craftsman, reflecting that the prayer was familiar and that the human mind has a tendency to read what it expects to see.

FYLINGTHORPE *Grid ref. NZ 937047*

—— In 1883, Squire John Walter Barry of Fyling Hall (now a school), at Fylingthorpe near Robin Hood's Bay, built a pigsty to house his two favourite sows; it is in an architectural style that is sumptuous and unusual to say the least. He obviously felt that his pigs deserved the best of environments, or perhaps he simply wanted an elaborate and whimsical folly to enhance the landscape on his estate. (Squire Barry often travelled abroad and came back with new architectural ideas, plants and trees.) For whatever reason, the pigsty was built in the form of a little Greek temple, complete with Doric columns and richly decorated in ochre, gold and red.

Whether the architectural glories of their dwelling, with its view to the sea in the distance, affected the eccentric squire's pigs favourably in any way we can never know, but they will surely add to the pleasure of present occupants, for the pigsty has been converted into a holiday home with all modern comforts and conveniences. No pigs included!

Inland from Fylingthorpe is Fylingdales Moor, where in 1961 the three domes of the Ballistic Missile Early Warning Station were installed, to become a gleaming white landmark, compared by many to giant golf balls. They have since been replaced by an ugly dull coloured pyramid with the top cut off, looking rather like a huge sandcastle.

Nearby is Lilla Cross, the oldest of the many moorland crosses, dating from the 7th century. Legend says that it commemorates the faithful attendant Lilla, who saved the life of

The piggery, Fylingthorpe.

Edwin, King of Northumbria. It was moved at one time away from the dangers of an army training area but is now returned to its original site.

GILLAMOOR *Grid ref. SE 682899*

The village of Gillamoor is situated on an escarpment on the southern edge of the North York Moors National Park and at the entrance to Farndale. The 'surprise view', for which Gillamoor is best known, comes into sight at a very sharp left turn in the road beside the church. It is best to leave the car behind and proceed on foot to the corner, which presents difficulties and dangers of stopping and parking, but this wonderful view looking down over the whole of Lower Farndale, beautiful in all seasons of the year, should on no account be missed. Its breathtaking beauty has inspired the inscription on the churchyard wall of a verse by John Keble, the 19th century Oxford professor of poetry and writer of hymns, after whom Keble College, Oxford is named.

'Thou who hast given me eyes to see
And love this sight so fair
Give me a heart to find out Thee
And read Thee everywhere.'

Whether religious or not, surely few could remain unaffected by the glorious panorama below.

The church too is of interest, being the work of one man, James Smith, who rebuilt it in 1802 entirely with his own hands. Designed to withstand the severe weather of the moors, it has no windows in its north and east walls.

The village also has a Methodist chapel, built in 1867 to commemorate two local men who helped to establish Methodism in America. They went in 1769, in answer to John Wesley's call for volunteer preachers to spread his word there. In those days this was a hazardous and difficult enterprise into the unknown undertaken by the two men – Joseph Pilmore from Fadmoor, a village less than a mile away, and Richard Boardman from Gillamoor itself.

In the centre of the village, set into a recess of the garden wall of Dial House Farm, is a rare sundial. It is of considerable size, consisting of a high stepped plinth and a central column, surmounted by a block with a dial face on each of its four sides. Sundials, the only instrument for telling the time before the invention of clocks, are of great antiquity, but since the clock came into use they have often been used to serve merely a decorative purpose. This one dates back to 1800 and was provided by public subscription, presumably as a memorial to someone or something. There is an inscription but I was unable to decipher it – perhaps others may do better!

GILLING EAST Grid ref. SE 615768

—— A stream flows beside the road and little bridges cross to the houses in the village of Gilling East in its beautiful setting at the foot of the Howardian Hills. As one passes through this charming village, Gilling Castle is hidden from view in the trees on the hillside above, at the end of a beech avenue almost a mile long.

Built as a fortified manor house by Thomas de Etton in 1349, it passed through marriage to the Catholic Fairfax family, becoming in 1929 the preparatory school for Ampleforth College. Its great tower is 70 feet high and 80 feet square, and the Great Chamber, designed and decorated by Sir William Fairfax in 1585, is one of the most impressive and resplendent Elizabethan rooms in England. After being stripped of its splendour in 1930, it was restored to its original condition in 1952, when the frieze, oak panelling, stained glass, ornate ceiling and splendid chimneypiece were recovered and reinstalled. Together with the lovely gardens and grounds, it can be viewed by the public on occasion in the summer months.

The clock on the tower of the village church was the gift of an Indian rajah, the famous Sussex and England batsman Prince Ranjitsinhji, who was the first player to make 3,000 runs in a season. When living at the rectory with a tutor he met at Cambridge, he played with the local cricketers on the green.

GOATHLAND *Grid ref. NZ 832011*

—— Clad with purple heather the North York Moors may look serene and beautiful, but the face they show is not always so kind. The unwary have been known to get lost on them, and in bad weather even those who know them well may find themselves in trouble. In a very bad winter of heavy snows moorland villages may become cut off. Indeed, Goathland, 500 feet above sea level and lying off the main road from Pickering to Whitby, has on occasion in the past been totally inaccessible by road for so long that food has had to be airlifted in.

In a setting of moors and wooded valleys the attractive village is spread wide, spaced out around large green areas dotted with grazing sheep. Once it was known mainly to the walking and hiking fraternity, who came to Goathland to enjoy the fresh air and scenery and admire the waterfalls in the neighbourhood, of which there are several. Probably the best of these is the 70 feet high Mallyan Spout, which is approached from the village by a steep path beside the Mallyan Spout Hotel.

Others, interested in history, came to visit the Roman road known as Wade's Causeway, on the moors nearby. It was uncovered in the late 1800s by James Patterson, a gamekeeper. Only a few slabs were revealed by him to visiting archaeologists, but now more than a mile can be seen. Its isolated position accounts for its survival and good state of preservation.

The rescue of the railway line by enthusiastic volunteers now brings tourists reliving the days of steam as they take the scenic ride from Pickering to Goathland in old style. So steep was the incline at one point that in the early days of rail travel the trains had to be hauled up it by cables, until the track was eventually rerouted.

Also, since the use of the village as the location for the television series *Heartbeat*, and the station's appearance as Hogwarts in the film of *Harry Potter and the Philosopher's Stone*, Goathland is no longer the quiet place it once was. It has become popular with ever more visitors, anxious to see the location, and hopeful possibly of seeing also filming taking place and the actors taking part.

One thing you can be sure they would *not* hope to see is the gytrash, also known as a padfoot, which tradition says haunted the countryside around Goathland, in the form of an enormous black goat, with eyes like red-hot coals and horns tipped with flames! The origin of the legend goes back to pagan times, when a wicked Lord Julian built himself a castle where Julian Park is today, and had a local maiden, Gytha, walled up in the foundations, thereby according to pagan belief ensuring protection from all enemies. For ten years he suffered after his evil deed, and the night he died the dreadful gytrash appeared for the first time.

It was said to be the ghost of Julian himself, doomed to continue to bring evil to the area, and its repeated appearances filled the whole countryside with terror, until a local witch cast a spell to drive it away. Fortunately she seems to have succeeded!

In his efforts to expiate his wrongdoing and free himself from his suffering, Julian is reputed to have built a chapel where the church now stands. The present church was built in Victorian times and fits well the character of the place. In the churchyard the grave of a master mariner and his wife is marked by a large ship's anchor, with its connotations of a ship brought to rest in safe harbour, and a reminder of the proximity of the Moors to the sea.

GRASSINGTON *Grid ref. SE 001636*

—— Though often referred to as a village, Grassington is in fact a small town, considered by many to be the 'capital' of

Upper Wharfedale. It was granted a charter as early as 1282 for a market and fair, which were still being held in the second half of the 1800s. Situated 700 feet above sea level and sheltered on the north-west by Grass Woods (a place of rare plants and butterflies, now owned by the Yorkshire Wildlife Fund), the town developed from an original settlement of farmhouses and outbuildings, many of the buildings seen today dating from the 17th century. Prior to the Enclosure Acts at the end of the 18th century, there were gates at the entrances to the town to keep out the animals. Towards the end of the 18th century, Grassington became a centre of the lead mining industry, when the Duke of Devonshire invested in the extraction of ore on Grassington Moor, and the town grew and prospered. Textiles, too, added to the prosperity of the place, until both industries declined in the 19th century.

Today, with its attractive cobbled square and narrow streets of grey stone cottages, Grassington is a popular, much loved tourist attraction. The old miners' cottages, unaltered in appearance – many still with their inglenook fireplaces and beehive ovens – are in great demand as holiday cottages. In the cobbled area of the square, near the pump that once provided the water supply, is the iron ring to which a bull would be tethered, a reminder of the barbaric baiting of animals which was enjoyed as entertainment in the past.

In 1766 Tom Lee, the notorious Grassington murderer, was executed at York Castle for the murder in Grass Wood of the local doctor. The old smithy where he lived is now a shop, but the place where his body was hung, on the site of the murder, is known to this day as Gibbet Hill. In Gars Lane, the side street running from the top end of the town to the square, look out for the little cottage named Theatre Cottage. It is on the site of the theatre where Tom Airey, the postmaster, presented his theatrical productions in the early 19th century. In 1807 Edmund Kean performed here, as well as Harriet Mellon, the little dressmaker who went on to become a famous actress and marry a duke. Long before they were applauded by the sophisticated theatregoers of London, they were appreciated here by an audience of farmers and lead miners, on a stage lit by candles. The Duke of Devonshire would occasionally grace the Grassington performances, seated in an opera box improvised from wood, and brown paper painted to look like curtains!

A special event nowadays, drawing many visitors in the winter, is the Dickensian weekend organised in the ideal setting of this delightful little town.

GREAT AYTON *Grid ref. NZ 557109*

───── With the reorganisation of local government boundaries in 1973, many Yorkshire people woke up to find themselves no longer living in Yorkshire. The people of Great Ayton, however, were having none of this, and when it seemed likely that they were going to become part of Cleveland, with true Yorkshire determination, they fought hard against it – and won! Living now in one of the most northerly of North Yorkshire villages, they celebrate their victory each year with a colourful gala.

The village has lost its many small industries such as milling and tanning and ironstone mining. In the 19th century so many miners flooded into the village that an area within it is still known as California, drawing a comparison to the famous Californian gold rush. Today it has become a commuter and dormitory village for the Cleveland industrial area, but above all it is famous as Captain Cook's village.

The great explorer was not born here but at Marton near Middlesborough, and at the age of eight moved with his parents to a Great Ayton farm. His old schoolroom is now a small museum, and an obelisk of Australian granite, like the one that marks the place of his first landing on the other side of the world, marks the spot where his parents' retirement cottage once stood. A rather poor exchange, one might think, for the cottage, which in 1934 was dismantled and taken to Australia to be re-erected in Fitzroy Gardens in Melbourne. When the cottage was offered for sale, the owner, faced by commercial offers from Americans, at first refused to sell unless it was guaranteed to remain in England. Eventually the Australian Agent-General came up from London and persuaded her to change her condition to 'not outside the Empire'. Painstakingly demolished, every brick or stone marked and numbered, it was shipped from Hull packed in 253 boxes. Even the creeper growing up the walls went too!

To the right of the path in the graveyard of All Saints' church is the gravestone of the explorer's mother and five of his siblings. It is sad to see that four of the children were less than five years old when they died, but it was by no means unusual for the times. The stone is thought to have been carved by

The Cook family gravestone, Great Ayton.

Cook's father and has an oddly expressed record of his brother William's age – 2 years 12 months 16 days and 7 hours. In contrast there seems to be some doubt as to the year of his death, which is given as 174$^7/_8$. The other side of the stone tells of Captain Cook's own death and shows an unusual spelling, to our modern eyes, of Hawaii, where he was killed, as Owhyee.

Long ago Great Ayton had a witch in the village known as Old Nanny. She is described in a dialect poem as being cross-eyed, with a long nose meeting her chin, pointed ears and a humped back. Although the poem accuses her of trading with the Devil, it seems likely that she was simply a poor ugly old woman, whose every action was misconstrued and whose mutterings were taken for curses and spells. The power of suggestion can make men believe many strange things.

GRINTON *Grid ref. SE 045984*

In medieval times the wicker coffins of the dead were carried from the distant corners of the dale along the Corpse Way to the nearest consecrated ground for burial. In bad weather, this was a dangerous undertaking and even in good it often took several days, necessitating stopping at places along the way for rest and refreshment for the pall-bearers and mourners.

The impressive church at Grinton, the mother church of Swaledale, sometimes called the Cathedral of the Dales, was at the end of that ancient way. But along the route to it the funeral party would meet with villagers in the dale, exchanging news and receiving condolences in the public houses in convivial style, with spiced ale, often drunk from special funeral mugs, and special funeral cakes to eat. At such places as Feetham and Ivelet Bridge, stone slabs can still be seen on which the coffins were rested.

It was customary in those days for the coffin of a shepherd to contain a sheepskin to identify him as such, so that he might be pardoned on Judgement Day for his unavoidably irregular attendance at church. In the 17th century, in order to bolster the wool trade, a law was passed making it an offence to be buried in any cloth other than wool. In 1692, when a certain Anne Barker was buried here in a shroud made of linen, the penalty paid by her father was a fine of five pounds – quite a considerable sum in those days.

An old three-arched bridge with projecting bays crosses the Swale at the entry to this ancient village, and the church, an inn and Blackburn Hall, the 17th century house of the lords of Grinton, cluster around it, while most of the houses are scattered up the gill. Like so many places in this area, Grinton was involved in the past in the mining of lead, and relics of the industry remain, including a smelt mill dating from about 1820, with a flue running up the hillside to carry the fumes away and a special store to keep dry the peat which was used as fuel for the furnaces.

GRISTHORPE *Grid ref. TA 083823*

There are newer houses behind it, but the old village street at Gristhorpe near Filey, some of its cottages more than 300 years old, has the serene air of a place that has been there a very long time. The whitewashed Bull Inn is the first building to greet one on the High Street, with the little white corrugated iron church of St Thomas actually attached to it. Opposite it is the attractive and imposing hall and at the far end of the sloping street, which ends in a public bridleway, the Manor House. Across the way from there, Manor Farm House has an interesting date stone over the door. At the top is the date 1665, with the initial B below, and also B and E. In a lower panel RB 1747 appears. A smaller stone on the house front tells us that it was restored in 1973 by Anelay of York. The Beswick family has long been associated with the village as landowners and lords of the manor; so it seems safe to assume a connection with the initials on the stone.

In 1824 William Beswick excavated a nearby ancient British barrow, and discovered a skeleton under some stones. In 1834, excavating a different tumulus, he again made the discovery of a body, together with weapons, a ring and other small items from the time of the early Britons. Within a hollowed out tree trunk, split to form a coffin and lid, was the perfectly preserved skeleton of a man measuring 6 feet 2 inches tall. He had been wrapped in an animal skin and placed in a foetal position in the coffin, which internally measured only 5 feet 4 inches. The skeleton was preserved and coloured by the chemical action of tannin and gallic acid in the tree trunk, and was covered by a fatty, waxy substance (adipocere), to which the flesh had been converted by water seeping into the coffin through a hole and under the lid. This tall well-built man, who now lies in the Rotunda Museum at Scarborough, was judged from the manner of his burial and the goods buried with him, to have had a position of some importance among the people of the Brigantes. It is known that Gristhorpe appeared in Domesday Book, but the exciting find of 'Gristhorpe man' indicates that there was a settlement here long before that.

HARDRAW *Grid ref. SD 864912*

——— Most visitors to this little place of grey stone houses, north of Hawes, head straight for the Green Dragon Inn, not necessarily to obtain refreshment – though they may well do that too, of course – but because the inn provides the only means of access to the path to Hardraw Force, England's highest waterfall. An abundance of waterfalls is a characteristic of the landscape of Wensleydale, which has been weathered into terraces with steps of steep little cliffs, or scars, down which the waterfalls tumble. This feature is due to alternating layers of shales, sandstones and limestone, which erode at different rates. Hardraw Force lies at the head of a limestone gorge and falls in an unbroken column for 100 feet from a rocky overhang, which makes it possible – though actively discouraged nowadays – to walk behind the falling water, as William Wordsworth once did.

This spectacular column of water, coming from a tiny tributary of the River Ure, has been known to freeze in severe winters, which must make it seem like a huge icy stalactite – a sight worth seeing. William Wordsworth and his sister Dorothy visited the fall in December 1799; John Ruskin was an admirer of it; and the great painter J.M.W. Turner made a painting of it. In a different kind of picture Kevin Kostner bathed and showered naked under it in *Robin Hood, Prince of Thieves*. It was a popular venue of the Victorians. The acoustics of the natural amphitheatre of the gorge are said to be excellent, and concerts and brass band contests were inaugurated there in the late 1800s, and have been revived in recent years. The great Blondin crossed the chasm on a tightrope one year, duplicating on a smaller scale his feat of crossing Niagara. He is said to have nonchalantly stopped halfway across to prepare an omelette.

There are other waterfalls in the woods above Hardraw Force but none can compare to it in spectacle and setting.

HARROGATE *Grid ref. SE 302552*

Harrogate is a town of flowers and trees. They are to be seen everywhere – in the busiest streets, in leafy squares and avenues and in parks and gardens with their beds and borders. The Stray, 200 acres of common land preserved for all time by an Act of Parliament, lies around three sides of the town and was once part of the ancient Forest of Knaresborough. In spring it is carpeted with gold and purple crocuses. It comes as no surprise to learn that Bishop Bickersteth of Ripon wrote the hymn 'Peace Perfect Peace' while sitting on the Stray one Sunday evening in 1876. Even with today's traffic it is possible to feel at peace there.

Yorkshire doctors were recommending the waters at Harrogate to their patients as early as Elizabethan times. William Slingsby had discovered the Tewit Well on the South Stray in 1571, but it was only with the greater accessibility afforded by improved roads, and then the coming of the railway in the 18th and 19th centuries, that Harrogate grew and flourished as a spa – or spaw, to use the old northern term – becoming ever more popular as a social as well as a remedial venue.

The Tewit Well is by no means Harrogate's only well. There are more than 80, many of them in Valley Gardens. They have different types of water – some sulphur, some chalybeate and some limestone – each supposedly with different curative properties. The sulphur water is said to be the strongest in England, and the taste has been described as 'bad eggs beaten up in paraffin' – nasty enough to cure anything – and it is still possible to check that out for yourself!

St John's Well on the Stray, beside the Wetherby road, was developed from a simple open air beginning into its present small but elegant building, though it catered for the less affluent with a free tap outside. The Royal Pump Room, now a museum, was built over the Sulphur Well, on which Harrogate came chiefly to depend, and, until their closure in 1969, the Royal Bath

Assembly Rooms housed a large hydrotherapy centre, treating among other things various rheumatic ailments.

Many famous visitors came to take the waters, William Wordsworth, Laurence Sterne and Charles Dickens among them. The satirical artist Thomas Rowlandson drew the Sulphur Well with one of the so-called attendant 'nymphs' handing out a tumbler of the water to his famous character Dr Syntax, while the gentry languidly look on. Betty Lupton became well known as the chief nymph, serving the public for 56 years. After taking the cure here, Louis Wain, the famous painter of cats, made an amusing drawing of cats taking the waters, accompanied by an orchestra composed of cats. Harrogate can lay claim to its own Victorian artist, William Powell Frith, whose pictures of crowded scenes in *Derby Day* and the *Railway Station* were to bring him renown. Although he was not born in Harrogate, he

St John's Well, Harrogate.

spent his youth in the town, where his father was the landlord of the Green Dragon Inn.

It is still possible in modern Harrogate to get a feeling of those more leisurely and elegant days of the past. Although no longer dependent on its waters, it is a popular conference venue, with a purpose-built conference centre. The Great Yorkshire Show is sited nearby and the town plays host to important antique fairs, a flower show and a toy fair.

If arriving in the town by train, or parking in the vicinity of the Victoria Shopping Centre, be sure to look out for the statues of ordinary citizens above it. It has been suggested that they look like would-be suicides about to jump, but they represent, of course, the people one might expect to find shopping below – a father with a child on his shoulders, a woman with a shopping bag, a middle-aged man in a raincoat.

HAWES *Grid ref. SD 875895*

A lively and busy venue for tourists – hikers, bikers, cyclists and motorists – yet still very much a farmers' market town, Hawes, the most important town of Upper Wensleydale, is situated at its eastern end and claims to be the highest market town in the country. Wensleydale is the home of the now rare Wensleydale sheep with its long lustrous soft fleece, and also of the cheese.

First made by monks in medieval times from ewes' milk, and beloved by cartoon characters Wallace and Gromit, Wensleydale cheese is eaten by all true Yorkshire men and women as an accompaniment to apple pie or Christmas cake. Today, at The Creamery on the outskirts of Hawes, it is possible to watch the traditional processes by which this queen of cheeses is made.

In the past the cheese industry here has gone through various vicissitudes. Its continuance owes a great deal to the foresight and determination of Kit Calvert, who rallied support to rescue the dairy when it faced closure in the 1930s. In 1992 the then owners of the business closed the creamery and transferred the production of Wensleydale cheese to Lancashire! Yorkshire outrage at this action resulted in a management buyout, and true handmade, as opposed to mass produced, Wensleydale cheese continues to be made in Hawes, the workforce including two of Kit Calvert's descendants.

Kit, who came to be known as the 'Father' of Hawes, had many interests, but above all the Dales, their history and dialects. He was a strong Methodist and translated the New Testament into the Wensleydale dialect. Noted as a great raconteur, antiquary and bibliophile, his bookshop in Hawes was a popular spot. It was not run for profit but for the love of books and learning. Often, it was left open and unattended, customers being trusted just to browse in its higgledy-piggledy disorder and to leave the price marked for any book that they took away. The Kit Calvert bookshop is still there, up a ginnel (alley) off the market place in Hawes, but sadly Kit himself is not.

Methodism and Quakerism both found a strong following in the Dales. Cockett's Hotel in the market place, once a Quaker building, has a splendid lintel over its doorway, dated 1668 and inscribed with the words 'God being with us who can be against'.

On a visit to the museum in the old station yard, be sure to pause at the top of the main staircase to enjoy the details in the beautiful embroidered collage hanging there, which depicts the story of the area. Trains no longer run to the station but one can still 'catch' one on the platform, its carriages containing some of the museum exhibits.

Should one leave the town by road in the direction of Bainbridge, a carved wooden wind vane beside a lay-by is worth looking out for. With a fish, ducks, a ram's head and a flower, it would seem to represent elements of the life of the Dales.

HAWNBY *Grid ref. SE 545895*

The route from Osmotherley to Hawnby, and ultimately to Helmsley, is one of the most thrilling and scenically beautiful in the whole of North Yorkshire. Climbing and descending, twisting and turning, it takes one through wild moorland dominated by the huge bulk of Black Hambleton, and through wooded areas and water splashes, before finally arriving at Hawnby on its steep hillside.

The village, with its red pantiled cottages, is built in two parts, at the top and bottom of the hill. This came about, so it is said, when two men working on the moors in the 18th century fell asleep in their midday break; amazingly, they both had the same dream calling on them to convert. As a result they sought out John Wesley, who was preaching in Newcastle, and were immediately converted to Methodism. On their return to Hawnby, however, when their conversion became known, they were evicted from their homes at the top of the hill by Lord Tancred, who was staunchly Anglican, and so they moved to the foot of the hill. In 1757 John Wesley visited the village and found a strong Methodist community established there. The old Wesleyan chapel, dated 1770, is still to be seen, complete with its old stove, pews and pulpit.

The 12th century church stands away from the village, hidden by trees on the banks of the River Rye. It contains many items of interest. A green man tops one of the pillars, and a painted memorial to little Ann Tankard, who died in 1608, shows her asleep in her cradle, a lily and a rosebush beside it, and a clock above, set between one and two to indicate the tender age at which she died. Three stained glass windows remember the surprising number of villagers who fell in the Great War, having been urged to join up by the rector known as 'the fighting parson of Hawnby', who himself lost three sons.

HAWSKER *Grid ref. NZ 925075*

Four miles south of Whitby, the A171 road from Whitby to Scarborough splits Hawsker into two parts, High Hawsker and Low Hawsker. High Hawsker has old stone cottages and the Hare and Hounds pub, while Low Hawsker contains more modern brick houses and bungalows. At one end of this part of the village, the whitewashed house of Mill Farm contrasts with the black-painted, truncated and sailless windmill that stands beside it and gives it its name. At the opposite end, a headless carved cross, thought to be the only relic of a chapel founded by Aschetil de Hawskesgarth during the reign of King Stephen, rises incongruously from the rows of peas and onions in a small vegetable garden. The cross can be viewed from both sides of the triangular garden plot, one side being the village street and the other a public footpath. A few yards down that public footpath, at the gateway of Hawsker Hall Farm, is a delightful, well-clipped piece of topiary in the form of a horse's head.

If one takes the road through High Hawsker, about a mile beyond it a plain nondescript little brick building can be seen at the roadside. It is worth stopping to look at it, for it contains Boiling Well, a spring which served the local community as far back as the 12th century, the time when the chapel was founded from which the ancient cross in Low Hawsker came. Like the well in the churchyard at Hinderwell, further up the coast (page 70), this one is associated with St Hilda of Whitby Abbey. Information on the structure covering it, however, tells us that in the early 19th century the water was carted to a reservoir at the abbey and from there piped to Whitby houses east of the River Esk, suggesting, perhaps, that the abbey connection may have originated as recently as that time. The name Boiling Well is not as one might suppose a reference to the temperature of the water, but to its bubbling emission, which still seems to be abundant.

HELMSLEY *Grid ref. SE 612838*

This market town on the River Rye, with roads from York, Thirsk, Stokesley and Pickering converging on it, is probably the most visited and popular in North Yorkshire. Whatever the season of the year Helmsley is always busy. Some visitors are there to look for a bargain on the market stalls, gathered on a Friday around the market cross and the elaborate memorial to the 2nd Lord Feversham, which stand in the centre of the square. On any day of the week, after browsing round the antique shops, the gift shops and the little art galleries, there are ancient pubs to enjoy and enticing tearooms. One such is the old police station, with its heavy cell door and home baked fare. Yorkshire curd tarts, known hereabouts as cheesecakes (or *chissacks* in the dialect) are a speciality not to be missed.

The ruined castle dominates the town. It was built by Robert de Roos, Lord of Helmsley, in 1186–1227, and in 1644 was held for three months against the Parliamentarian forces led by Sir Thomas Fairfax of Gilling. After its surrender Parliament ordered it to be dismantled beyond use, but its interesting architectural plan, with the keep built into the outer wall, can still be seen.

Duncombe Park, the seat of the Earl of Feversham, is also in Helmsley. Built in 1713 by an amateur architect named Wakefield, in the style of Vanbrugh, who built Castle Howard, it was twice damaged by fire but rebuilt in the original style. The house, gardens and parkland are now open to the public from April to October, after many years' occupation by a private school for girls. In a stroll along the woodland walk, keep a look out for the tallest ash tree in England; it stands beside the path and is marked by a plaque. The main feature of the gardens is the long grass terrace with a small Greek temple at either end. One is Doric, the other Ionic, the latter being decorated as an elegant dining room and open to view. Once a favourite picnic place for the Feversham family, the terrace looks down onto the River Rye and gives a dramatic view of Rievaulx Abbey below. This was the first Cistercian monastery in the north of England. The Reverend Grey, vicar of Helmsley from 1870 to 1913, had a wild ambition to rebuild Rievaulx Abbey but had to abandon the scheme when he was unable to raise the £30,000 needed at the time. How much would it cost today I wonder! He did succeed in establishing the tradition of an annual service in the ruins, and designed the mural in Helmsley church. The abbey can be reached by a 2-mile walk along a footpath from the car park in Helmsley, or from the village of Rievaulx.

It is worth taking the road past the church and the Feversham Arms, and then following the gated road to the left, marked 'No Through Road', for about 4 miles to Helmsley Bank, for the splendid views and lovely scenery. These are to be expected in this area of special beauty, but more of a surprise is the piece of modern sculpture isolated out here in the countryside. The work of the York sculptor Austin Wright, it was installed in 1977 to a chorus of protests, and much conflicting opinion and controversy in the local papers. Some people denounced the modern design while others deplored its location, yet the simple large empty frames of the sculpture contain and focus the eye on parts of the surrounding scenery and seem eminently suitable in the countryside, while the contrast between nature and the man-made object highlights and enhances the visual pleasure of both.

HELPERBY *Grid ref. SE 440698*

—— Helperby, though a modern thriving community, is a village that visually belongs to an earlier age. Indeed, so complete is this period air that the village was chosen a few years ago as the location for a television costume drama about the early 19th century poisoner William Palmer. Its cobbled main street and fine old houses provided a ready-made authentic background, and the villagers enjoyed their brief moments of fame as extras.

Helperby Hall, a Queen Anne residence which has belonged to the Milnes Coates family for many generations, is an attractive feature of this altogether attractive village. The imposing domed well or fountain standing in the main street was provided by the Coates family in 1897, in commemoration of Queen Victoria's Diamond Jubilee, and was, until the 1930s, the water supply for the village. Though no doubt a boon to the villagers at the time, it is a reminder today of a hard life, when water had to be carried in buckets.

Turn the corner at the end of the main street, and one is in the village of Brafferton. It is older than Helperby, having been a Saxon settlement as early as the 7th century, whereas Helperby was built at a later date by the Vikings. But even though it may be able to claim seniority, Brafferton has not quite the old-world charm of its sister village.

HINDERWELL *Grid ref. NZ 796166*

—— The village of Hinderwell lies along the main Whitby to Loftus road, about a mile inland between Staithes and Runswick Bay. It does not have the picturesque attractions of those two coastal villages, but the traveller who pauses there instead of hurrying through will find that it has interest of its own. In particular it contains the feature that is said to have given the village its name. At the northern end of the village the church stands high on a triangular island of green surrounded by roads, and in the churchyard, not instantly distinguishable from the gravestones, is St Hilda's Well. It is not the type of well with a deep sunken shaft, but a spring or fount welling up from the sloping ground and protected by a table-like construction of stone slabs.

St Hilda, who was Abbess of Hartlepool, founded the abbey at Whitby in AD 657 and was its abbess until her death in 680. One legend says that she had a cell at Hinderwell, where she could retire for meditation, but another claims only that she rested here and refreshed herself at the well on her journeys through the area. Corruption over the years of the words *Hildar wella*, giving eventually the name Hinderwell, seems plausible, but, whether you believe in the legends or not, it is not too difficult in the quiet graveyard, with traffic out of sight and hearing, to imagine the abbess refreshing herself at the well and blessing it. As with many such wells, there have been in the past claims of curative properties for the water, and as happens in Derbyshire the well is annually dressed with flowers by the children of Hinderwell.

A plaque on the well states that it was restored in 1912 by Hilda Palmer of Grinkle Park, a reminder of the important influence of Sir Charles Palmer. He had extensive ironstone mining operations in the area in the 19th century and built the little harbour at nearby Port Mulgrave in order to ship the ore to his furnaces in Jarrow. In 1865 he bought the Grinkle Park estate and came to live there, later purchasing an adjoining estate which included the village of Hinderwell.

In 1828 the miller Isaac Moon built a windmill seven storeys high in the village. In 1870 it was converted to steam, but ceased operation around the turn of the century, and its machinery was removed in 1915. It must have been an impressive sight, but sadly nothing remains of this huge and magnificent building today.

HOLE OF HORCUM *Grid ref. SE 845935*

No matter how many times one has seen it, something still draws one to one of the most astonishing sights in North Yorkshire. If the weather is fine the lay-by about eight miles from Pickering on the road to Whitby is rarely empty, as motorists stop to view the wonderful natural amphitheatre that is the Hole of Horcum. Cameras and binoculars appear and mothers keep tight hold of little ones as they stand on the edge of this awesome green bowl and gaze into its 300 feet depths. It is a surprising geological feature to find in this landscape, which is more generally convex in its contours than concave. It might seem to be man-made, but was in fact formed thousands of years ago by the effects of water erosion.

Of course one may prefer the more fantastic version that says it was the result of a domestic incident between the local Giant Wade and his wife Bell. It seems he was in such a rage with her that he scooped up a handful of earth and threw it at her, but missed, being no doubt too cross to take careful aim, and the result was the Hole of Horcum and the hill known as Blakey Topping some distance away. Wade and his wife are given credit for quite a few achievements around these parts. The Roman road on Wheeldale Moor near Goathland is known as Wade's Causeway, supposedly built so that Bell could drive her cows along it over the boggy ground. And she and Wade, so we are told, built Pickering Castle and Mulgrave Castle near Whitby, tossing their only hammer over the 20 miles between them, as the need arose!

Whichever explanation you favour, it is undeniably a spectacular view and must be an exhilarating experience for the hang-gliders who can sometimes be seen hovering and swooping down into it.

HORTON-IN-RIBBLESDALE   *Grid ref. SD 808726*

The wide open spaces of Ribblesdale lie between the peaks of Ingleborough (2,373 feet) and Pen-y-Ghent (2,273 feet), with Whernside (2,414 feet) beyond at Ribblehead. Horton-in-Ribblesdale's typical dales houses, long and low with slate roofs, are built from the limestone quarried in the area. Situated at the foot of Pen-y-Ghent, the village is the base for the classic and popular 25-mile circuit of the Three Peaks Walk; its successful completion within 12 hours is rewarded with a badge. As a safety measure walkers book in at the Penyghent Café before setting out and report back on their return. Such is the popularity of the challenge that conservationists are worried about the erosion caused by so many feet, and duckboards have been placed on some of the pathways.

A little further up the dale, in the north slope of Ingleborough, is Alum Pot, probably the most famous of the many potholes in this area. Surrounded by trees, it is 130 feet long, 40 feet wide and 292 feet deep. About 100 feet down it is crossed by a natural bridge of limestone, and to one side Alum Beck descends in a waterfall. Some 150 yards away is Long Churn Cave, an underground passage, which emerges into Alum Pot a little distance above the limestone bridge. It is often used by potholers as an entry – though not an easy one – to Alum Pot in preference to descending by rope-ladder. In 1936 there was a fatal accident in Alum Pot, caused not by the accepted dangers of potholing but by a stone, thoughtlessly thrown down from above, which struck a resting potholer below.

Perhaps the best known and most conspicuous feature of the dale is the Ribblehead Viaduct, carrying the Settle-Carlisle railway line across Batty Moss before it enters Blea Moor Tunnel. With its 24 stone arches, the viaduct is $1/4$ mile long and more than 100 feet above the ground. Its foundations were finally successfully laid in the boggy ground only by the use of innumerable sheepskins as a base. The building of the railway was a remarkable feat of Victorian engineering in difficult terrain and wild weather. It took seven years to its completion in 1876, at a cost of £3,467,000 and a heavy toll in the lives of the navvies building it. They came from all parts of the country to work on it, often bringing their families with them to live in shanty towns with names such as Batty Green, Jericho, Sebastapol and Salt Lake City. The largest, Batty Green, with two thousand inhabitants, was unusual in having a school, a mission house, a post office, and a hospital to care for the victims of an epidemic of smallpox in 1871. A memorial at the church in Chapel-le-Dale, where many of them are buried, remembers those who died in building the railway. Looking at the empty and desolate landscape where these rough townships once stood like gold rush towns, it is difficult to visualise them and the hardships, drunken brawls and personal tragedies that once took place in them.

The weather in these parts is ever an important factor. Wind has been known to be so strong as to stop trains. Though no doubt apocryphal, a story is told of a man who was blown off the viaduct at one side, through the arches and back on to it at the other side!

In the 1980s there was talk of closing the line, but strong protests and vigorous campaigning won the day, keeping this line over some of the most lonely and magnificent scenery open, to be enjoyed by tourists, ramblers, railway buffs and locals as before.

HOVINGHAM *Grid ref. SE 669756*

—— If we take the old Roman road out of Malton to Helmsley, we come to the attractive village of Hovingham, its stone cottages clustered around the green and a stream running through. It lies in a beautiful setting of hills and trees, the latter once part of the ancient Forest of Galtres. In the early 1800s it was hoped to develop the village as a spa, based on the medicinal springs discovered nearby. Although the project never really got off the ground, the railway station – now defunct of course since Dr Beeching – always bore the name Hovingham Spa.

Hovingham Hall, built on the site of a Roman villa, stands at the heart of the village behind Hall Green. It was the home before her marriage of Katherine Worsley, now the Duchess of Kent, and was built between 1752 and 1769 by Thomas Worsley, Surveyor General to King George III, to an unusual and idiosyncratic design. Thomas Worsley was passionately fond of horses and was recognised as one of the best riders of his day. He planned his house in such a way that his horses were housed within it, on the ground floor. The front door is reached through the riding school and leads, not as one might expect into an elegant hallway, but directly into the vaulted stables.

A balcony off the grand ballroom, which is above the stables, overlooks the riding school, and guests in all their finery could have the extra diversion of watching the horses below. To Thomas Worsley with his great love of horses, no doubt the horsy noises and smells were a pleasure, but one does wonder whether this unusual arrangement with rooms of the house over the stables might not have had its disadvantages – especially in hot weather! The hall is not open to the general public, but the riding school is used for music concerts, and open air village events overtaken by bad weather. Cricket matches, where many famous players have appeared, take place too in the grounds of the hall.

One should be sure to notice the extraordinarily large oriel window on the village school opposite the hall. It was described by Sir Nicholas Pevsner, the famous commentator on British architecture, as 'truly hideous'. Others may well consider it merely unusually opulent and quaint.

HUBBERHOLME *Grid ref. SD 928785*

Buckden Pike, at 2,300 feet high, and the fells rise like walls on both sides of Hubberholme, lying far up the valley of the River Wharfe. The main features of this lovely spot are the public house, the rugged grey 12th century church and the old stone bridge connecting the two.

Each year the ancient Hubberholme Parliament meets in the George Inn to auction the so-called poor pasture behind the inn in aid of the old people of the parish.

J.B. Priestley, the Yorkshire author, loved this place. His ashes are buried in the churchyard on the opposite bank of the river, and a memorial remembers him in the church. Until the late 15th century Hubberholme church had no rights of burial, and corpses had to be carried across rough hilly tracks for burial at Arncliffe. It was only after a corpse was swept away in the raging River Wharfe and eight bearers perished in snowdrifts that burial rights were granted. The great treasure of the church is the rood loft, one of only two remaining in Yorkshire, the other being at Flamborough on the coast. It would seem that the Diocese of York, to which it belonged, forgot the existence of Hubberholme, tucked away in the dale, and so it escaped the edict of 1571 for the removal of its beautiful rood loft. The little mouse on the more modern woodwork of the pews shows it to be the work of Robert Thompson of Kilburn, one of his earliest commissions, installed in 1934.

Thomas Lindley, curate of Halton Gill, crossed Horse Head Pass between 1802 and 1833 in all weathers to take services at Hubberholme. A window in the church shows him making the journey on a white horse in the winter snow. When he was expected, a watch was kept by a man on the roof of one of the houses until he was sighted. Only then was the church bell rung and the congregation assembled. Another curate, Miles Wilson, in 1743 wrote a story about a man going to the moon from the top of Pen-y-ghent. His object was to teach astronomy but he could perhaps be said to have written the first space adventure.

HUNMANBY *Grid ref. TA 097777*

The Wolds slope down gradually to Filey Bay and Hunmanby Sands. The village of Hunmanby, set back from the shore, caters for its seaside visitors without any of the brashness of the large resorts. It has a caravan park, a farm holiday village and a craft centre, and the village streets offer a variety of shops, ranging from a family butcher to antique shops. You may spot a shop with the intriguing name Jalopies' Jaunty Collectibles!

On the edge of the village, Hunmanby Hall, once a Methodist school for girls, is now converted to luxury apartments. The church of All Saints and the Methodist chapel are both very large. In front of the modern looking chapel, on a little green, stands a very weathered and battered ancient stone cross in a fenced enclosure.

Along the long street named Stonegate, to the right beyond the Horseshoe pub and on the corner of Sheepdyke Lane, are the village lock-up and pinfold adjoining each other on the village green. A notice tells us that the lock-up was erected in 1834 and was often needed after the annual fairs, when too much indulgence in alcohol caused disorderly scenes. Here the villagers who strayed from the straight and narrow could be held until they sobered up, or could be handed over to a higher authority. Similarly straying animals were held in the pinfold next door until handed over to their owners upon payment of a fine to the pinder – one of the many occupational names incidentally, that have given rise to surnames. The lock-up has two very small cells with narrow doors and tiny barred windows, offering less spacious accommodation and apparently no more comfort than the adjacent circular pinfold (built from cobbles from the shore), but having at least the advantage of a roof.

Is it just coincidence, I wonder, that Stonegate leads to Pinfold Green, where cobbles carted from the shore were once broken up by stonebreakers for use in the making of roads?

HUTTON-LE-HOLE *Grid ref. SE 703900*

A beautiful village in Ryedale and the North York Moors National Park, Hutton-le-Hole draws tourists like bees to a honeypot. Its stone cottages, with red pantiled roofs, are built at all angles around a large green which is close cropped by black-faced moorland sheep. Hutton Beck flows through a deep cleft in the green, crossed by little white wooden bridges. Until the

The witchpost, Hutton-le-Hole.

Dissolution of the Monasteries, Hutton-le-Hole was owned by St Mary's Abbey in York. In the past it was involved in the ironstone industry of neighbouring Farndale and Rosedale.

It was always a strong centre of nonconformism, both Methodist and Quaker. The Quakers formed a small community working as weavers. Look out for a cottage with the inscription JR 1695 on it. It was here that John Richard, a Quaker and a friend of William Penn, lived. He began to preach at the early age of 18, riding his white horse thousands of miles through America, where he once took part in a council of white men and American Indians. At the end of his travels he returned to the peace and quiet of Hutton-le-Hole, where he died in 1753; he was buried at Kirkbymoorside. Another inscription, scarcely to be missed, is a stone with the words, 'By Hammer and Hand all Arts do Stand', and the initials of Emmanuel and Betty Strickland. This is on the house which they built as an inn in 1784.

The admirable Ryedale Folk Museum, founded in the early 1960s by Bertram Frank, tells the history of the area and forms almost a small village within the village, consisting as it does of many local buildings, which have been dismantled, transported, reconstructed and furnished to give a realistic impression of local life, crafts, customs and trades over many years. A longhouse, a cruck cottage and a great hall are among the buildings that can be seen there. A witch in her hovel reminds us of a period that believed in witchcraft and the power of witches, perhaps especially in remote rural areas.

Witchposts seem to be a feature almost exclusive to the North York Moors. Of the 19 known examples, only one – from Lancashire – has been found outside this area. In addition to the example housed here at the museum, in a cruck cottage from Danby (see page 41), other witchposts have been found at Farndale, Rosedale, Gillamoor, Egton and Lealholm. There may be others as yet undiscovered, for as recently as 1984 a cottage on sale near Pickering was found to contain one. Built into the structure of the cottage, usually to support the smoke hood above the fireplace, they were carved from oak or rowan, trees traditionally credited with magical properties. Their distinguishing feature is a cross carved near the top, together with other symbols, and sometimes a date from the 17th century.

Despite their traditional name, however, there is no irrefutable evidence to support the idea that their purpose was to protect the house from witches. As the 17th century was also a time of religious intolerance, it has been suggested that itinerant priests may have been sheltered in the cottages, and the occasion recorded by carving a cross.

ILTON *Grid ref. SE 190785*

—— If you take the road from the town of Masham through Swinton and Ilton, and a mile beyond Ilton decide to take a stroll in the Forestry Commission woods, you can be 'sure of a big surprise'. Not, as the song has it, a teddy bears' picnic, but, tucked away in a clearing, silent and secret, a druids' temple. The approach to it is lined with standing stones, but it is still a surprising sight; one is quite unprepared to come upon what appears to be a smaller version of Stonehenge. It was built in about 1800 as a folly. There was a great interest at that time in both follies and druids, and after a tour on the Continent, where he had seen an original temple, William Danby (1752–1833) of Swinton Hall was inspired with the idea to build something on his estate, giving work to unemployed workmen and paying them one shilling a day.

By the beginning of the last century it had become a popular place for picnics and chapel outings. Today it is a quiet and unusual place to visit, after a pleasant walk through the woods, with a lovely view to contemplate beyond it, overlooking the nearby reservoir.

JERVAULX ABBEY *Grid ref. SE 172857*

—— The ruins of Jervaulx Abbey, on the banks of the River Ure between Middleham and Masham, show very clearly the ground plan of this great Cistercian abbey, though standing remains are few. The ruins are open to the public and it is interesting to note the huge kitchen, considering the frugal diet of the monks. Until the 15th century they were allowed no meat, cheese or eggs unless they were ill, only bread and vegetables cooked without fat. The abbey was founded in 1156 by monks from Byland who had struggled for several years with the hardships of a bleak site at Fors near Askrigg, until, according to legend, they were led by a vision to the site of Jervaulx. They were granted the land by the Earl of Richmond, and the abbey became one of the most important and richest in Yorkshire, with income from iron and coal mining and large flocks of sheep. The monks of Jervaulx are credited with being the first to produce Wensleydale cheese with the milk from their ewes, as well as being the first to breed horses and exercise them on the Middleham moors – both traditions still carried on in the area.

In 1536 the Abbot of Jervaulx, Adam Sedbergh, much against his will and under threat to his life, joined the ill-fated Pilgrimage of Grace on the journey to London, hoping to compel or persuade Henry VIII to spare the monasteries. The King offered to pardon the pilgrims for their insurrection but in fact took his revenge. Jervaulx, like all the other monasteries, was destroyed in 1537, and Adam Sedbergh, convicted for his part in the pilgrimage, was beheaded at Tyburn. His name and the date 1537 are still to be seen carved into the wall of Beauchamp Tower in the Tower of London, where he was held before his execution.

KILBURN *Grid ref. SE 512794*

Kilburn is a small attractive place lying in the shadow of Roulston Scar, which is a part of the Hambleton Hills. It has a small stream running through it, with little bridges across to the gardens of the cottages, some of which are old and timbered. To those who know it, two animals spring instantly to mind at mention of the name – one large, one small; one a landmark, the other a trademark. The first is the white horse, measuring 314 feet long and 228 feet high, which is cut into the 1-in-4 escarpment above the village, and the second is the little mouse carved on every piece of work that leaves the workshop of the famous woodcarver Robert 'Mousey' Thompson in the village below.

The horse, naturalistic in appearance, is not of prehistoric origin like that on the Berkshire Downs above Uffingham, though it was inspired by it. It was the idea, after seeing the Uffingham horse, of Thomas Taylor of Kilburn, who had left his native village to make his fortune in London. Taylor found an ally in John Hodgson, the village schoolmaster, who drew up the plans and supervised the construction. The task was completed on November 4th 1857, and was celebrated with a great feast, when more than 100 gallons of beer were drunk and two roasted bullocks were eaten.

The horse is cut on limestone, which does not give a more or less permanently white surface as chalk does. Six tons of lime were originally used to whiten the surface and frequent resurfacing is needed to keep its colour. Over the years different materials have been used, from chalk chippings to special paints, but the steepness of the hill makes restoration a very difficult task. Visitors today are discouraged from walking on it, although picnics on the eye of the horse, which can accommodate 20 people, were once popular. The horse is said to be visible across the Vale of York from as far as 40 miles away.

Many intaglio hill-horses were cut in the 18th and 19th centuries but few of them remain. The Kilburn White Horse is a unique feature in the north, and the long association of the Hambleton Hills with horseracing makes its siting particularly appropriate.

Kilburn's other animal, the little wooden mouse of Robert Thompson (1876–1955) can be seen not only in Yorkshire – or even Britain – but in all corners of the globe. He is said to have adopted it as his trademark when a fellow carver remarked that they were 'as poor as church mice', but his work was to become so famous that a letter sent from the other side of the world, addressed simply with the drawing of a mouse and the words 'Woodcarver, England', arrived at his workshop.

Kilburn. The white horse and Robert Thompson's mouse.

The son of the village carpenter, Robert was sent as an apprentice to a firm of engineers in the West Riding. On his regular journeys home, he visited Ripon Cathedral and was inspired by the work of William Bromflet, the founder of the Ripon School of carvers. Unable to settle to town life or engineering, Robert returned to work with his father in Kilburn when his apprenticeship was over. Gradually from there he built up his reputation as a carver, noted for his true craftsmanship and perfectionism.

Today his work is carried on by his great-grandsons, and a small museum to his memory has been opened in the old joiner's shop where it all began. When Professor Josef Heu, an Austrian woodcarver of repute, fled with his family from Hitler's persecution and made his home in nearby Ampleforth, Robert Thompson offered him work at Kilburn. As a tribute to his fellow craftsman, Professor Heu carved a portrait plaque, which hangs in the museum. This lovely piece of work shows Robert Thompson as the rugged, straightforward, unpretentious Yorkshireman that he always remained, though his works are to be seen in palaces, churches and many high places.

With a touch of humour, Professor Heu has carved a somewhat strange looking mouse – or could it be a lizard? – crawling up Robert Thompson's sleeve!

KILDWICK *Grid ref. SE 008461*

Just outside the Yorkshire Dales National Park, skirted by the busy main road between Skipton and Keighley that once went right through it, the village of Kildwick lies, peacefully now, against the northern hillside of the Aire valley. A bridge built in the 14th century by the canons of Bolton Priory crosses the river into the village, while the Leeds-Liverpool canal cuts through it and crosses over the road to the neighbouring village of Farnhill. Well into the 20th century the canal was busy with barges carrying goods to and from the spinning and weaving mills in the area, but the textile industry no longer flourishes and the mills have been taken over for other uses. Brightly coloured barges and other boats are still to be seen on the canal, but today they provide pleasure trips and holidays.

The church of St Andrew, approached up steep stone steps, dominates the village from its elevated site. The first impression of the church itself is of its great length. It is mainly of the 14th century, but at some period the choir was extended to a length of 170 feet, thus earning the church the title Lang Kirk o' Craven. During the Crimean War the people of Kildwick received a letter from Florence Nightingale at Scutari thanking them for their help with her work. I understand that it is kept in the church, but sadly, like so many in today's dishonest times, the church is kept locked.

However, one should not leave without seeing a very unusual memorial in the churchyard. Turn left at the church door, then left again across the church car park to see the gravestone of John Laycock, who died in 1889 aged 81. He was an organ builder from nearby Glusburn, and his memorial is a copy of the first organ that he built. It is naturally smaller than the original – indeed smaller than one might expect, and so easy to miss – but unique and interesting in its detail, and very different from the bland uniformity of modern gravestones, which tell us little about the character or interests of those who lie beneath them.

KIRBY HILL *Grid ref. SE 388685*

—— Roads have always been important in the history of the area around the village of Kirby Hill, which lies about a mile from the town of Boroughbridge. The Roman road named Dere Street ran through it from York to the north, and later the Great North Road, from London to Edinburgh. Kirby Hill lies at the exact mid-point between the two capitals on that once busy road, as shown on the old milestone which stands partially hidden in the hedge beside the Blue Bell inn. This attractive and popular old hostelry was a busy coaching inn in the 18th century. There are said to be iron rings still evident in its cellar, where prisoners were once chained overnight, on their way along the road to trial or prison in York. Today the A1 takes the heavy traffic, bypassing Kirby Hill, to the great relief of the village.

KIRBY WISKE *Grid ref. SE 374846*

—— There are many place names in Yorkshire ending with the suffix -by – meaning 'village', 'farmstead', and indicating a former Danish settlement – and many variations of Kirkby ('village with a church'). Kirby Wiske, situated four miles north of Thirsk and just off the A167, is further distinguished by the affix *Wiske*, indicating that it lies close to the River Wiske, which flows into the Swale.

It is known as the birthplace of Roger Ascham (1515–1568), the English classical scholar who became secretary and Latin tutor to both Queen Mary and Queen Elizabeth. In 1545 he published *Toxophilus*, a treatise on archery, which he dedicated to Henry VIII, who rewarded him with a pension of £10 a year. However, the latter years of his life were marred by poverty and anxiety about the future of his wife and family.

The church of St John the Baptist, standing on a raised area in the village, has an interesting Norman doorway with an arch of grotesque animal heads. Inside is a memorial to Fanny Isabel, the wife of Francis Samuelson, who was the son of a wealthy 19th century industrialist. She was the mistress of Sion Hill Hall nearby. She was preparing for a social occasion, either by candlelight or perhaps using curling tongs, when her hair caught fire and she died from her burns. She was pregnant at the time, and it would appear that her unborn child died with her. This tragic and unusual event is commemorated by the beautiful sculpture of a woman nursing two children. It is the work of Sir George James Frampton RA, who sculpted the statue of Queen Victoria in Calcutta, and of Edith Cavell in London. The inscription is in Latin, but the story is told in translation beside it.

Sion Hill Hall, replacing an earlier building, was designed in 1913 by the talented York architect Walter Brierley, who was known as the Lutyens of the north. This lovely country house, considered by many to be his masterpiece, is not a great imposing stately home, but a house which one feels would be a comfortable place to live. It is owned today by a charitable trust and is open to the public from Easter to the end of September. It houses a collection of china and furniture, and has the added attractions of demonstrations of birds of prey in the grounds, a teashop and gift shop in the stable block, and a collection of old bicycles and baby carriages.

KIRKBYMOORSIDE *Grid ref. SE 696865*

Kirkbymoorside is an attractive grey-walled and red-roofed historic market town on the edge of the North York Moors, and is a popular venue for tourists. The weekly market in the town's spacious square draws custom not only from locals and nearby villagers but also from further afield.

In this largely agricultural landscape flax was once a very important crop, and the part of the town known as Kirkby Mills was where the spinning and weaving of linen was carried on. Now only the name remains as a reminder of the industry.

To the north of the town are the few surviving traces of the castle of the Nevilles, who lost their estate here for rebellion against Queen Elizabeth I. It was later given to the Duke of Buckingham by James I.

In April 1687 George Villiers, 2nd Duke of Buckingham, was taken ill while hunting on the moors. He was carried into Kirkbymoorside, into the town's 'best house', where he died. He had once been a great wit and a favourite of Charles II, but had fallen from grace. After losing his influence and great wealth, he had restored and lived in part of nearby Helmsley Castle, leading an empty life of pleasure and frittering away the days with drinking, dancing and hunting – a sad end for a brilliant courtier of enormous power, who having offended or quarrelled with everyone, died alone and forsaken in this small Yorkshire town, weary of the wasted life he had been leading.

The house where he died is still there. Known ever since as Buckingham House it faces the old tollbooth – now the Memorial Hall – across the market square. The church register records the death of 'George Vilaus lord dook of bookingham'.

KIRKDALE *Grid ref. SE 695865*

To reach this little dale you turn off the A170 between Helmsley and Kirkbymoorside. It has neither village nor hamlet. The road takes you through a ford, and into the lovely valley of Hodge Beck, where the little grey church that is St Gregory's Minster, stands in tranquil and romantic isolation. Indeed, so quiet is it, that death watch beetle was said to have been discovered in the church at one time by the sound of the insects' champing jaws alone!

In the Vale of Pickering many old churches have stones of Celtic and Saxon origin built into them, but St Gregory's has the great treasure and unique feature of a large, well-preserved Saxon sundial inside the porch over the south doorway. It is 7 feet long and 2 feet wide and divided into three panels. Interestingly, the dial in the centre panel is divided into an eight-hour day. Above the dial an inscription reads, 'This is the day's sun marker at every time'. The inscriptions are not difficult to understand despite the Northumbrian English and some runic characters. The wording of the side panels, translated into modern language, says, 'Orm Gamal's son bought St Gregory's Minster when it was all broken down and fallen and he let it be made new from the ground to Christ and St Gregory in the days of Edward the King and Tosti the Earl. And Harwarth me wrought and Brand priest.' These names and information make it possible to date the building and sundial to between 1055 and 1065.

Retracing one's steps to the ford and an old quarry nearby brings one to Kirkdale Cave, which was discovered in 1821, when workmen found bones and teeth. They supposed that they

The sundial, St Gregory's Minster, Kirkdale.

were those of cattle that had been buried there, but one man, John Gibson, appreciated the importance of the find, and Professor Buckland, an expert from Oxford University, was called in. In the cave behind the quarry face the remains of as many as 300 hyenas were found, and with them the remains of other animals, including rhinoceros, lion, hippopotamus, elephant, mammoth and reindeer. The discovery of what was in fact a prehistoric hyena den was startling proof of large and ferocious animals roaming the English countryside in the prehistoric period, and it caused great excitement at the time. Today the quarry is overgrown and the cave little more than a narrow fissure.

As well as the hyena den, which measured 300 feet long, it is believed that a system of caves may exist in this area, which would also perhaps explain the occasional disappearance underground of Hodge Beck, which flows on one side of St Gregory's graveyard. According to legend, a duck once walked underground from Kirkdale Cave to Kirkbymoorside two miles away. But did it take the Underground or did it fly, we ask ourselves!

KNARESBOROUGH *Grid ref. SE 355575*

Where do hundreds of people every year take a walk along a wooded riverbank to look at gloves and shoes, teddy bears and other strange objects of stone? The answer is of course the ancient and picturesque town of Knaresborough on the River Nidd, near Harrogate, their destination the dropping or petrifying well, probably the best known of the town's unusual attractions. Such are the minerals in the water dropping over the rock that any articles hung beneath are gradually turned to stone.

Mother Shipton, Knaresborough's famous prophetess, was born in 1488 in a cave close by this unusual water, and no doubt she used it in the herbal cures for which she became noted. The illegitimate daughter of Agatha Sonteil, Ursula was deformed as a child by arthritis and left an orphan to fend for herself at an early age. At 24 she married a man named Toby Shipton and was known thereafter as Mother Shipton. She was a clever herbalist and noted for her healing powers, but above all she was renowned for her prophesies, many of which appear to have come true, though it seems that some were not hers, but attributed to her in the 19th century. She did predict with complete accuracy the date (1561) of her death. If you place your hand in the water of the 'well' in the corner of her cave and make a wish, they say your wish will be granted. It works (well my wish came true!), but only if you let your hand dry naturally.

Another cave dweller in Knaresborough was St Robert, who lived the simple life of a hermit in his cave beside the Nidd, on what is now called Abbey Road. Although he was known as St Robert, the title was unofficially given in tribute to the holiness of Robert Flower. Born in 1160 of a well-to-do family in York, he chose to live in Knaresborough on bread and herbs, wild berries and roots, begging for alms, which he used to help poor prisoners. He was famed not just locally but throughout Europe for his healing skills and wise advice. He died in 1218, outliving by two years King John, who had visited and consulted him when in the town, and granted him a piece of land on which a priory was later built. We can appreciate the peace and quiet of his bare and lonely cave, but hardly imagine the harshness of his life there, without even the basic creature comforts that we take for granted. In the 18th century the notorious murderer Eugene Aram buried his victim in St Robert's cave, where it lay undiscovered for many years.

In 1770 a weaver by the name of Thomas Hill set to with his son to dig out a house from the solid rock face. The Duchess of Buccleuth gave financial aid to the project, and, after 16 years of work with only hammer and chisel, the four-storey building was completed. It was named Fort Montague in honour of the duchess, who visited it many times. It must surely be one of the most unusual dwellings in the country and was happily lived in until recently. Nearby is yet another building hollowed out of the solid rock. This is the shrine of Our Lady of the Crag, once known as St Robert's Chapel. Its doorway is guarded by the carved figure of a knight drawing his sword. It is believed to date from around 1190 and to have been where St Robert prayed. A different story claims that it was carved out in gratitude by a local stone mason called John, on the spot where his son was miraculously rescued alive after being buried by a fall of rock. The chapel is rather tucked away, with a house almost in front of it on Abbey Road, but is well worth seeking out.

This enchanting town on its rocky hill, a ruined castle crowning the summit, has a jumble of houses and gardens rising up from the deep gorge which the river flows through and which is spanned by a high-arched and battlemented railway viaduct. Knaresborough is full of surprises and is deservedly popular with artists and visitors. Should you be there at carnival time in the month of June, a highlight of the attractions is the bed race, when entrants from near and far push their 'beds' of all descriptions through the streets of the town and the river as well!

LANGTHWAITE *Grid ref. NZ 005025*

Arkengarthdale branches out from Swaledale in a northerly direction at Reeth, and Arkle Beck runs down the little valley for 11 miles before joining the Swale near the village of Grinton. Langthwaite is the principal village of the dale, along whose length lie hamlets with unusual and evocative names such as Arkle Town, Booze, Eskeleth, Whaw, Wham and Windegg.

Like Swaledale, Arkengarthdale was from Roman times bound up with the lead mining industry, with the addition here of both coal mining and quarrying for chert. In 1656 the valley was purchased from the citizens of London, to whom it had been sold by King Charles I, by Dr John Bathurst, physician to Oliver Cromwell, and the connection of his family to the dale lasted until 1912. In 1657 Dr Bathurst founded a school in Langthwaite. Although autocratic, he took a personal interest in his tenants and the men who worked in his mines; he sent them tobacco from London, and paid a shilling each quarter to impoverished widows, on condition of their attendance at church. The mines were carried on by his son and then his grandson, both named Charles Bathurst, who gave their name to the C.B. Company and the C.B. Inn.

Surrender Smelt Mill in Arkengarthdale is a reminder of the dale's past industry, but perhaps a more curious and interesting relic is to be seen standing in the middle of a field, to the right of and beyond the C.B. Inn. A hexagonal building, that could be mistaken for a small chapel, it is in fact a powder house, built in 1804 for the C.B. mines, to store the gunpowder used to blast the rock in order to extract the lead. Because of its extremely unpredictable and volatile nature, it was necessary to store the powder well away from any habitation. Nevertheless, this substance had to be used by the miners, working by candlelight in the confined space of the mine tunnels – often with tragic results.

LASTINGHAM *Grid ref. SE 725905*

'Among lofty and remote hills, more suitable for the dens of lurking robbers and retreats for wild beasts than the habitations of men.' That is how the Venerable Bede, in his *History of the English Church and People*, described Lastingham (or Laestingaeu as it was then known), the wild and desolate place in which St Cedd of Lindisfarne, Bishop of East Anglia, chose to build a monastery in AD 659. Cedd fell a victim to the plague, died, and was buried there. He was followed as head of the monastery by his brother, St Chad, who later became Bishop of York and Lichfield.

In the 9th or 10th century the monastery was destroyed, in all probability by the Danes, but in 1078, Stephen, Abbot of Whitby, set out to rebuild it. He built the crypt as a shrine to St Cedd, who lies buried beside the altar. The apsidal crypt is unique in the country, the only surviving example with a chancel, nave and aisles – a small church in itself. The Whitby monks were not long at Lastingham, leaving to found St Mary's Abbey in York because of the danger from marauders, and the monastery was never completed. The present church was built in 1228 on the foundations of Stephen's abbey church. It is an awe inspiring experience today to stand in the peaceful crypt where those ancient saints have been – yet, according to legend, cock-fighting took place in it in the 18th century!

Opposite the church is the pub, which in the 18th century was kept by the vicar's wife. With 13 children it was very necessary to eke out the vicar's stipend of only £20 a year. However, the Rev Jeremiah Carter was brought before the ecclesiastical authorities and reprimanded for playing the fiddle for dancing in the pub between Sunday services. His defence that dancing prevented young people from drinking too much seems to have been accepted and he was excused on account of his circumstances, but his stipend was not increased.

A plaque in the village commemorates the artist John Jackson, who was born in Lastingham in 1778, the son of an itinerant tailor. His talent was recognised even as a boy drawing his schoolfellows, and with financial assistance from a wealthy sponsor he was sent to the Royal Academy and later to Italy to study. From his humble beginnings, he rose to become a Royal Academician in 1817; he lived in London, where he made a good income as a famous portrait painter, but because of his generosity he never became a rich man. Perhaps bearing in mind the help that had been given to him, he felt that he too should help others. Although he was a Methodist, he painted and presented to the church at Lastingham, a copy of Correggio's *Agony in the Garden* as an altarpiece. He died in London in 1831.

There are three holy wells in Lastingham dedicated to St Cedd, St Chad and St Ovin; they were once part of the village water supply.

Before you leave this lovely village, lying in its hollow between moors and woodland, look out, men, for this warning message carved above a doorway:

'The hap of a life
Good or ill
The Choyce of a wife.'

LEYBURN *Grid ref. SE 115905*

When in 1563 the plague struck the market town of Wensley, which gave its name to the dale, many of the people fled to Leyburn, a hamlet high on the bank of the River Ure, thinking it a more healthy place to be. As Wensley dwindled and lost its status, Leyburn grew and prospered. It was granted a charter for markets and fairs in 1684, and by the 1800s its population had doubled. There are many pleasant buildings in this mainly Georgian and Victorian town but perhaps the most architecturally imposing is Leyburn Hall, dating from 1750. The town has three spacious squares, the largest of them being Market Square, which is surrounded by shops and cafés and inns, busy with visitors drawn by the lovely countryside, and farmers and their wives in town for the markets and cattle auctions. The typical Victorian drinking fountain in Market

Square is worth looking out for but may easily be missed amongst all the hustle and bustle and parked cars.

Also in the square, the Black Swan, once the corn exchange, bears an unusual 'decoration' displayed on its frontage. A 200-year-old mantrap is a reminder of the horrendous means landowners were prepared to use against trespassers and poachers. These vicious traps were sprung when trodden on unawares. Their metal jaws, clamped round a man's leg, could break it or seriously mutilate it.

Round the corner, in the High Street, is the house where Frances I'Anson, the 'sweet lass of Richmond Hill', was born in 1766. The initials of her grandfather and the date 1746 can be seen above the door. Frances married Leonard MacNally, an Irish lawyer, who immortalised her in his love song. How could any woman resist!

Leyburn also has a connection with another romantic subject, but in this case it is a tragic one. It was here that Mary, Queen of Scots was recaptured after her escape from Bolton Castle, where she was in the custody of Lord Scrope and Sir Thomas Knollys. A lane leading off Commercial Square takes one onto The Shawl; this is a natural terrace, almost two miles long, along which Mary tried to escape with the aid of a young guardsman who had succumbed to her charms. Legend says that it was here that she dropped her shawl, thus giving a name to this place with its wonderful views across the Wensleydale countryside.

LINTON-IN-CRAVEN *Grid ref. SD 995625*

——— Grey stone houses and cottages cluster round a large green sloping gently down to Linton Beck, in the pretty little Dales village of Linton-in-Craven. Should you wish to visit the white-walled pub at the top of the green, the little stream offers various ways to cross it. There is the clapper bridge (a bridge formed from one flat length of stone) towards the southern end of the green, the elegant 14th century packhorse bridge, or the modern road bridge. Alternatively, there is a shallow ford that you could wade across, or stones in the beck that could be used as stepping-stones – though that might be an unwise choice on the return from the inn!

Reminders of the flax grown in the fields around and spun by the village women until the 18th century are to be found in the village in the shape of large stone troughs. These were filled with water and used to rot the flax in order to obtain the fibres for spinning.

Overlooking the green is the imposing building of the Fountaine Hospital, which was provided by money left in the will of Richard Fountaine, who died in 1721. He left Linton as a young man in 1660 to seek his fortune in the capital. He caught the infection in the Great Plague of London in 1665 but recovered and was given the official job of organising the disposal of the victims. He became an alderman of the City of London and a wealthy man, leaving his fortune to provide an almshouse for three poor men and three poor women of Linton. The design, though there is no actual record of the architect, is said to be by Vanbrugh, the architect of Castle Howard near York. It is most unusual in its grandeur for such a tiny village.

Linton's church, a long low building with features from as early as the 12th century, is not in the village itself. Surprisingly it stands almost a mile outside, down by the River Wharfe, at the centre of a network of footpaths from the several villages and hamlets that it serves. There are stepping stones crossing the river nearby, but the Wharfe, as is typical of Dales rivers, can rise very rapidly after rain, and they are only passable when the water level is low.

LINTON-ON-OUSE *Grid ref. SE 496607*

In the years immediately prior to the Second World War airfields were quickly being constructed all over the country. Many sprang up on the suitably flat lands of the Vale of York, surrounding the city of York on all sides. During the war airmen from the Dominions and Europe were stationed on these Yorkshire fields: Canadians, Australians, Free French and Poles, as well as members of our own air force. Heavy bombers droned nightly across the skies from Linton-on-Ouse to their targets in Germany. The construction of the airfield there in 1936 brought great changes to this previously wholly agricultural village, taking over farmland and several farms, but bringing with it work of a different kind. After the war many of the airfields were abandoned, or developed or converted to peacetime uses. Linton-on-Ouse, however, still remains an RAF station today and an important element in the life of the village.

The unexpected name of the village inn, The College Arms, may puzzle the stranger seeing it here in this small country place and wondering to what college it could refer. The explanation lies back in 1706, when the village was sold by its owners, the Appleby family, to Queen Anne's physician, Dr John Radcliffe. He bequeathed it to University College, Oxford, the rents of the farms and cottages to fund two scholarships for medical students.

The road through the village and past the aerodrome takes one to the toll bridge at Aldwark. On the way a parking and viewing area is now thoughtfully provided for fans to see the planes where once notices forbade one to stop. In the opposite direction, off the road between Linton and its neighbouring village of Newton, a track leads down to the River Ouse and the lock and weir constructed in 1767 to facilitate the carrying of goods up river by barge. Today transport by river is a thing of the past, though there are suggestions of reviving it as a 'green' method of relieving congestion on the roads. Meanwhile the lock is devoted to pleasure, as the popular Linton Locks Marina.

LITTLEBECK *Grid ref. NZ 846007*

There are many waterfalls on the North York Moors and one of the loveliest is the 50 feet high Falling Foss in the wooded valley of the prosaically named Little Beck. Above the waterfall and only 20 feet away, Midge Hall was built by the landowner Sir James Wilson as a cottage for his gamekeeper – with an outside toilet emptying over the waterfall! One wonders what it was like to live there outside the village, tucked away in the woods, with primitive facilities and the constant sound of the waterfall.

Less than a mile away from the waterfall is the Hermitage, a large boulder hollowed out to form a shelter with a gothic pointed doorway and stone seating. It was the work of a sailor named Jeffery for the local schoolmaster, George Chubb, whose initials and the date 1790 appear over the doorway. This man-made cave is an example of the 'follies' that were popular at the

The Hermitage, Littlebeck.

time, and was part of a scheme to enhance the grounds of nearby Newton House for its new owner Jonas Brown.

The road to Littlebeck is twisting and precipitous, taking one down from the moorland road between Pickering and Whitby to this little village in a secluded valley that once provided oak trees for the shipyard at Whitby. It was an ideal spot for smugglers to hide out, and there are also signs of more legitimate activity in the remains of abandoned jet and alum workings. In a much earlier age the monks from the abbey at Whitby had a chapel hospitium here. The land at Littlebeck owned by the Abbot was let to the Prior of Bridlington, who was allowed to graze 20 mares and their foals, at an annual rent of a pound of wax and a pound of incense, to be paid at Whitby on St Hilda's day (St Hilda was the founder of Whitby Abbey in AD 657). The hospitium eventually became an inn and then a private house, though symbols of its past can still be seen.

LYTHE *Grid ref. NZ 845135*

———— Lythe means 'slope', and the long steep hill known as Lythe Bank climbs from Sandsend to the village, 500 feet above sea level, giving magnificent views over the sea and countryside, and across the bay to Whitby. The church of St Oswald, standing high on the hill just before the village, is a landmark visible for miles around from both land and sea. Anglo-Danish stones in the church come from a Danish graveyard, where settlers were buried following the Viking landing near Lythe in AD 867. Also in the church are two ophicleides, which the musically knowledgeable will be aware are rare obsolete musical instruments. They were once used in the church to support the singing in the choir, and it is well worth seeing these large black wind instruments, if only to marvel at how anyone could play anything looking so heavy and clumsy or to imagine the kind of sound they might make.

Mulgrave Castle, home to the Phipps, Earls and Lords of Mulgrave, lies on a wooded slope to the south of the village. Henry Phipps, 1st Earl of Mulgrave, spoke against the abolition of slavery, on the grounds that he had never seen slaves ill-treated, but by an ironic coincidence it fell to Sir Charles Phipps, as Governor of Jamaica, to travel around the plantations in 1832 informing the slaves of their freedom. Another member of the Phipps family had the task of paying out compensation to the slave owners. The 2nd Baron Mulgrave, Constantine John Phipps, was a sea captain who had as a midshipman amongst the crew of his vessel the young Nelson.

An old custom in Lythe known as 'firing the stiddy' is used to mark special occasions in the village, such as visits from royalty or other dignitaries, weddings and births at Mulgrave Castle, or village festivals. The blacksmith's anvil is brought out and upturned on the common; a charge of gunpowder is placed in it and detonated using a long metal bar heated red hot at one end. The village pub, once The Red Lion, is now called The Stiddy and has a sign illustrating this strange old custom.

MALHAM *Grid ref. SD 905625*

———— Considering its size – only 11 miles long – Malhamdale, with its dramatic limestone landscape, is probably the most striking of the Yorkshire dales. It was generally believed that the spectacular Malham Cove, carved out by glaciers and waterfalls, was formed during the last Ice Age, which ended about 14,000 years ago. Recently, though, a Leeds University scientist has presented evidence that the feature must in fact be four times older than was thought – dating back 50,000 years or more. Topped by a limestone pavement, this awe-inspiring curved cliff of limestone, about a mile north of the village of Malham, is nearly 1,000 feet wide and almost 300 feet high. The massive waterfall that fell from it in the far distant past would have been higher than Niagara. The water trickling from its base is popularly supposed to be the source of the River Aire. The novelist Charles Kingsley stayed with his friend Walter Morrison, a millionaire industrialist, at Malham Tarn House (now a field centre), and it is claimed that the house, the white limestone scenery streaked with black moss, and the characters he met on his visit were the inspiration for his book *The Water Babies*. The bells ringing in Tom's ears as he came down to the river only to fall asleep and begin his adventures as a water baby we can suppose to be those of Malham church – the church where the signature of Oliver Cromwell appears twice in the parish registers as witness to a marriage. Since Cromwell is known to have visited in the area, they could well be authentic.

Malham Tarn, from which Morrison's house on the north bank took its name, is high on the moor two miles north of Malham. It is one of only two natural lakes in the Dales, the other being Semerwater. It lies 1,229 feet above sea level, is 14 feet deep, and is of particular scientific importance because of its lime-rich nature.

While Malham Cove has been described as a 'dry waterfall', Gordale Scar, a deep narrow gorge with precipitous limestone cliffs, about a mile north-east of Malham, is usually thought of as a collapsed cavern. However, it may have been carved out by the action of glacial meltdown. Gordale Beck, pouring through a hole at the top of the cliff face at the end of the gorge, creates two waterfalls. Whatever the cause of this dramatic feature of the landscape, it has long been – and continues to be – a source of inspiration to artists. It has been the subject of paintings by Turner and John Piper, and visited by Ruskin, Darwin, and William and Dorothy Wordsworth. Early tourists declared themselves 'horrified' by the great limestone cliffs and 'savage' landscape around Malham. Thomas Gray, after visiting Gordale Scar in 1769, wrote to a friend telling of a goat on the cliffs that 'danced and scratched an ear with its hind foot, in a place where I would not have stood stock still for all under the moon'.

Today's tourists seem to have no such fears, making Malham one of the most visited places in the Dales.

MALTON *Grid ref. SE 785715*

—— There is a saying in Malton that digging down one spit will produce a Roman urn and two spits a Roman pavement! Not strictly true, of course, but nevertheless the little museum in this market town contains a wealth of Roman remains: coins, stone balls used in catapults, arrow heads, spurs, beads, painted wall plaster, sandals and domestic utensils. Some were found in archaeological digs, but some were uncovered purely by accident, like the huge storage jar unearthed by the vicar digging in his garden. As the fortified Roman station Derventio, Malton was at the centre of a network of highways stretching inland to York and to the signal stations established along the Yorkshire coast.

There are two parts to the town – Old Malton and (New) Malton – and its sister town of Norton is divided from it only by the bridge over the River Derwent. Old Malton has thatched cottages and an old inn, and the magnificent church of St Mary with its great tower, which was once part of the 12th century Gilbertine priory. In the churchyard is the grave of Charles Smithson, one of Charles Dickens' greatest friends, who lived three miles from Malton, and died aged only 39. Dickens loved this area and was a frequent visitor to his friend. It was Smithson who helped him to concoct a story of an imaginary boy as a ploy to enable him to visit the schools on which he based his Dotheboys Hall in Nicholas Nickleby.

Nothing remains of the Norman castle which once stood here, or of the great house that succeeded it in 1600, except a high stone wall with archways. Behind it is the Old Lodge, now a hotel, part of which is old and part modern. And thereby hangs a strange tale! The old part is reputed to have been built from the stone of the great house, which is said to have been demolished in Stuart times when two heiresses quarrelled over it. Since they could not agree, they were ordered by the sheriff, in a Solomon-style verdict, to take down the house and divide the stones between them.

A vaulted crypt underneath the Cross Keys Hotel in Wheelgate is connected with the priory in Old Malton. It is all that remains of three hotels in the district, founded about 1150 by Eustace Fitzjohn, who was also the founder of the priory. They were maintained by the canons of the priory as a hostel for travellers, pilgrims and the homeless.

The church of St Michael stands in a block of buildings (including the town hall) which divides the market place into two parts. As well as the general market there is also a flourishing cattle market, but the old Shambles is now given over to little shops selling antiques, books and knick-knacks, and the two breweries that the town once had no longer fill the air with the smell of hops.

In 1933 Malton was hit by an epidemic of typhoid, in which the doctor, Dr G.C. Parkin was struck down by the disease, at the age of 31, after devoting himself, untiringly and regardless of risk, to caring for his patients. He is buried in the cemetery, an unsung hero of the town.

MARRICK *Grid ref. SE 075985*

—— The railway, though considered from time to time, never actually came through Swaledale, making it somewhat inaccessible in the past. But today's motorist has the choice of two roads from Richmond to Reeth: the old road on the north of the river and the 'new' road to the south. Marrick lies a mile off the old road west of Richmond and 1,000 feet above sea level.

Just before the crossroads to Marrick and Hurst, a lane leads to the ruins of Marrick lead smelting mills, for this now quiet village was, like so much of Swaledale, once at the centre of the lead mining industry. As far back as Roman times, lead was mined here, and in the 16th and 17th centuries some of the most profitable mines in the area were developed at Marrick by John Sayer, a wealthy Roman Catholic squire from Great Worsall. His profits were as much as £1,000 a year, enabling him to pay £260 a year as a fine for not worshipping as an Anglican. The 19th century saw the decline of the industry because of foreign imports, and in 1890 Low Mill – one of the earliest in the Dales – and High Mill were both closed.

Marrick Priory, a Benedictine nunnery founded in the 12th century on the north bank of the River Swale, is reached from the village down a steep bank by a stone causeway known as the Nuns' Causey. Consisting of 365 flagstones it was constructed, according to local tradition, by laying one flag each day for a year. It does seem highly unlikely, for what purpose could such a slow rate of progress serve? Another, more romantic story is attached to the priory. It tells how Isabella Beauford, maid of honour to Catherine of Aragon, fled from the lecherous advances of Henry VIII and sought sanctuary here. She was sheltered by the nuns until Henry's death in 1547, whereupon the story ends with her return and marriage to her true love, Edward Herbert, a Somerset squire. However, a burial stone in the chancel of the priory for 'nun Isabella, sister of Thomas Pudsey de Barfort' has been claimed by some to be that of Isabella Beauford. If this is indeed the Isabella of our tale, it seems that it did not have a happy ending after all.

Very little of the priory remains today. It is not open to the public but can be seen from footpaths and distantly from the B6270 road. Only the church tower is original, the rest having been re-erected in the 19th century.

MASHAM *Grid ref. SE 225805*

—— A huge cobbled square with trees and flowers and a market cross with a base of five well worn steps form the central feature of Masham. Visitors come here not only for the charm of this Wensleydale market town by the River Ure, but also to visit – and sample the products of – its main industry. The Theakstons of Masham can trace their family tree back to the 15th century, a fact which is true of many families still living in the Dales. It was in 1875 that they built their brewery here, though they had practised brewing long before that, behind the Black Bull inn. There are now two breweries in the town, with a visitors' centre and conducted tours. Serious beer drinkers will no doubt know their most potent brew, Old Peculier – no, that is not a spelling mistake but a name from Masham's past. It commemorates the town's ancient status as 'a peculier'. That meant that it was independent of the diocese in which it lies, giving its church council special rights within the parish.

At the end of September Masham holds its sheep fair, an event that goes back a long way. It was once a great event lasting three days, with farmers from all over the Dales and drovers from as far away as Scotland and Ireland filling the square and the streets with sheep and cattle. It was not just an agricultural occasion but also a great get-together for the Dales folk, in the days when contact was not as easy as it is today.

Masham is not all beer and sheep, however. In 1804 an artist with the spendid name of Julius Caesar Ibbetson came to live here, spending the last eight years of his life in the town, where he did some of his best paintings. He was a popular and kindly man, who involved himself in the community and took an active interest in its development. On his gravestone, on the north side of the church in Masham churchyard, he is described as 'an artist eminent for his taste and skill in painting rustic figures, cattle and rural scenery'. His pictures are on show in many municipal galleries, as well as the Victoria and Albert Museum and the British Museum. His life was rather unkindly summed up by the

The Square, Masham, as seen from the King's Head Hotel.

famous art critic R.H. Wilenski in the words: '... went to China, returned to London, wrote a book on painting, took to drink, became enormously fat and died in the village of Masham.'

MIDDLEHAM *Grid ref. SE 126876*

The Richard III Hotel and the Nosebag Teashop, right next door to each other on the steeply sloping market square, illustrate the two main claims to fame, past and present, of the township of Middleham in the Yorkshire Dales. It was here that Richard of Gloucester, later to become Richard III, lived for many years and here that his son Edward was born in 1473. Married to Anne Neville, the daughter of the Earl of Warwick, Richard was a power in the north, keeping law and order and defending the region against the Scots. He gained much respect in Yorkshire as a good, far-sighted and courageous leader, and despite his later character assassination he is still held in high regard in the county. In 1934 the Richard III Society provided a stained glass window to his memory in Middleham's church of St Alkeda. Richard had made the church collegiate and it remained so until 1856, Charles Kingsley being one of the last of its canons. A dean at one time turned the town into a kind of Gretna Green by performing marriages without either licences or the calling of banns. Richard loved Middleham but left for the south, eventually to become King, returning only once, on the early death of his son.

Though the town is mostly Georgian, its most prominent feature is surely the ruins of Richard's great castle, with its historic connections. It was built around 1170 and is now in the care of English Heritage.

At the top end of the town the old school, church-like with its Gothic tower, proclaims its new use as a bookshop-gallery by means of an interesting and unusual sculpture that stands before it. Like a gnarled and twisted tree trunk, its stark whiteness stands out against the grey walls. Also worthy of note is a house with a very large sundial on it. Middleham has two market squares and here, in the Top Market, is the old market cross, known as the Swine Cross. It is in two parts, and it is said that deals were finalised by a handshake in the space between. On one of the blocks, so very much eroded by time and weather as to be barely recognisable as an animal, is what may be a representation of the boar of Richard III or perhaps the bear of the Warwicks.

The name of the hotel in the market square is plainly explained by the town's historic connections, but what of the teashop? 'Nosebag' is a witty reference to the great importance of the horse in this centre of racehorse breeding and training, which was made famous when local trainer James Croft's horses took the first four places in the 1822 St Leger. Today about a dozen training stables around the town stable horses equalling in number almost half of the town's human population. Every day the horses are taken for exercise to the gallops on Middleham Low Moor. In the late 18th century horse races were being held on the moors and the first racing stables were established, but long before that the monks of Jervaulx Abbey were training their horses there.

Opposite the all-weather training track, before the turning to Melmerby on the Wensley to West Witton road, is a small brick building with empty doorways which declares itself the old Rubbing House. This is where the horses were rubbed down after coming off the gallops and, although not used since 1870, yet if you venture to look inside, you will find that it still smells of horses.

To approach Middleham from Leyburn one crosses the River Ure by a bridge with medieval-looking castellated towers. Originally one of the country's earliest suspension bridges, it was built in 1829 by Joseph Hansom, the inventor of the hansom cab. It collapsed as a herd of bullocks crossed it, causing fateful vibrations when by chance they fell into step, so we are told. That must have been quite a sight – a herd of bullocks marching in step! It was subsequently converted to an iron girder bridge but it still has the towers which once held the suspension cables.

🍂 MOOR MONKTON   *Grid ref. SE 508568*

▬▬▬ Some five miles west of York, a quiet side road leads off the A59 to the small riparian village of Moor Monkton, situated in a cul-de-sac at the confluence of the rivers Nidd and Ouse. Across the Nidd is the village of Nun Monkton and across the

Ouse is Beningbrough, both near neighbours but neither accessible without returning to the main road.

In 1999 this small community of less than 300, with help from a lottery grant, funded and refurbished the old schoolroom to provide a new village hall for the new millennium.

In 1640 Sir Henry Slingsby rebuilt Red House, his home outside the village, in the style of Lord Holland's Kensington House in London. During the Civil War Red House was a centre of support for the King against the Parliamentarians and it was here that Sir Henry was captured and led off to execution in 1658. While York, just those few miles away, was in the hands of the Parliamentarians, Sir Henry was in hiding in a secret room at Red House, but one day, feeling the need for exercise and a breath of fresh air, he unwisely took a stroll in his grounds, only to be spotted from across the Ouse by Sir John Bouchier of Beningbrough, who betrayed him to his enemies.

On an interesting and unusual staircase, removed from the house during a Victorian restoration and installed in the chapel, each newel post bears the crest of a Royalist supporter and friend of Sir Henry. They are the Pembroke wyvern, Bethell eagle, Vavasour cock, Stapylton hound, Fenwick phoenix, Belasis stag's head, Savile owl, Percy lion, Fairfax lion's head, and the lion and leopard of Slingsby himself. Also on the stairway is the rather battered figure of a little black boy who originally held a candlestick in each hand to light the stair. It is reputed to be the earliest lead statue in the country and was the work of a Dutchman, Andrew Karne.

The Jacobean chapel, unusually for a family chapel, is not within the house, but stands very close to it. Until the recent closure of the school which had been at Red House for many years, it was still in use as the school chapel, and open to the public.

MOORLAND CROSSES

There are many ancient stone crosses on the North York Moors, indeed they are such a feature of this area that one of them – Ralph Cross, called Young Ralph to distinguish it from Old Ralph – has been adopted as the symbol and logo of the National Park. Many are medieval in origin, but their purpose is shrouded in mystery. Some would seem to be marking the boundaries of parishes or other territories, while others may be waymarkers intended as guides to travellers on ancient routes across the moors. Whatever their purpose, they are an enigmatic presence standing solitary on the empty moors.

The oldest of all the moorland crosses is Lilla Cross, which stands on the prehistoric track known as Old Wife's Trod, above Lilla Howe, and dates from the 7th century. According to legend, the King of the West Saxons sent an assassin in AD 626 to kill Edwin, King of Northumbria, whose kingdom stretched from the Scottish borders down to the Humber. As Edwin journeyed across Fylingdales Moor, the assassin struck, but his faithful attendant Lilla saved Edwin's life by interposing his own body and taking a fatal blow from a poisoned sword. The cross is a memorial to Lilla, who was a Christian.

White Cross, Old Marjery, Old Ralph and Young Ralph also have their legends. Young Ralph stands 1,400 feet above sea level, high on Westerdale Moor, at the crossroads to Castleton, Hutton-le-Hole and Rosedale. A few hundred yards to the south-west is the smaller cross known as Old Ralph. White Cross is known familiarly as Fat Betty, on account of its appearance, being a squat white stone with a wheel top; it marks the conjunction of the parish boundaries of Danby, Rosedale and Westerdale. Old Marjery is not far away.

It is said that Old Ralph was a lay servant attached to the 11th century nunnery at Rosedale and served as a guide across the moors to the sister convent at Baysdale. One day he was escorting Sister Elizabeth from Rosedale to a halfway point where she had arranged to meet Sister Marjery of Baysdale to settle a problem regarding boundaries. Caught in a sudden roak (a local name for a thick sea fog), they became lost, and Ralph told Sister Elizabeth to wait beside a stone while he set out to find Sister Marjery. Cold and lonely, she waited and prayed beside the stone for several hours, until the fog lifted and she was able to see Ralph and Marjery only a few hundred yards away. The three points were then marked by the crosses named by Ralph as White Cross (after Sister Elizabeth's robes), Old Marjery or Marjery Bradley and Old Ralph.

Young Ralph probably dates from the 18th century, replacing a 13th century boundary stone. The story of this cross says that it was erected by a local farmer on the spot where a poor traveller

Fat Betty.

had died from exhaustion, in order to provide a guide and sustenance for travellers. At the top of the nine feet high cross is a hollow where money could be left by those who could afford it for less fortunate wayfarers. At such a height one wonders how anyone could reach the hollow either to place the offerings or to retrieve them. Indeed, the cross has been broken in recent times, on more than one occasion, by those attempting to check the hollow to see if anyone following the ancient custom had left any money. As a result Young Ralph now faces the world with a metal rod carefully and cleverly inserted down his middle.

❧ MOUNT GRACE PRIORY   *Grid ref. SE 452985*

Mount Grace Priory is signposted on the A19 less than a mile beyond the turning to Osmotherley, and is situated at the foot of the Cleveland Hills, against a wooded background. It was founded in 1398 and is the largest and best-preserved of only nine Carthusian monasteries in England. The life of the monks of the Carthusian Order was one of manual work, prayer and study, isolated from the outside world and for the most part from each other. This way of life is shown very clearly at Mount Grace Priory. The monks met only in the church and ate together in the frater only on festival days. Communal rooms such as dormitories were consequently not a feature of Carthusian monasteries as they are of others. Instead individual cells, or small houses, were ranged around the cloisters, each containing a living-room, a bedroom, a workshop and a study, with a small herb garden behind. At the end of the garden a small closet was set over the main drain.

Emphasising the solitary and silent nature of their life are the hatches beside the doors along the cloister, through which food was passed to the monks inside. Without a door, but making a right-angled bend in the thickness of the wall, the hatch enabled the server to place the food and the monk to retrieve it, without the possibility of either catching so much as a glimpse of the other. Speaking was forbidden except on Sundays, but it must surely have been hard to resist a stolen whisper through the hatch. One wonders how often the food, placed silently within, grew cold when the inmate, perhaps deep in prayer and meditation, did not realise that it was there.

Following the Dissolution of the Monasteries, the guesthouse of the priory eventually became a private house in 1654, and in 1900 came into the possession of the Bell family. Gertrude Bell (1868–1926), the traveller and archaeologist, spent her childhood here, and visited whenever possible as an adult. She was known as the 'uncrowned queen of Arabia' and her knowledge of the area was invaluable in the First World War. Today the building is owned by the National Trust and in the care of English Heritage. A monk's cell and garden have been fully restored to the state in which they would have been when occupied, and though it is small and simple many visitors are heard to say, 'I wouldn't mind living in this myself!' The accommodation might well be acceptable but the isolation and lack of companionship would be a different matter altogether for most people, I feel sure.

MYTON-ON-SWALE *Grid ref. SE 435466*

—— In the rural peace of the quiet cul-de-sac of red-roofed cottages that is Myton today, it is difficult to imagine that it was once the scene of a gruesome and bloody battle.

In the 1300s Myton and its lands belonged to the Abbey of St Mary in York. In 1319 during the Scottish battle for independence, when the Scots, led by the Earl of Murray and James Douglas, advanced as far as Myton, they were met by an army of clergy and civilians, sent out by the Archbishop and the City of York to block their passage and protect the Queen, who was at the time lodged in York (a strange idea to have an army of clergy, surely?). Though the Scots lost few of their men, the nearby River Swale was clogged with bodies, and Myton Pastures were white with the vestments of slaughtered priests, the engagement thus becoming known as The White Battle.

From 1615 until 1933 the Myton estate was owned by the Stapylton family. The lovely hall is said to have been built in 1630 and enlarged in 1693. It was occupied by the Stapyltons until it was requisitioned for use as a convalescent home during the Second World War. It was sold in 1946 to a man who had made his fortune building wartime airfields, and is now owned by a supermarket magnate, who has on occasion opened the grounds to members of the public in aid of charity, having lovingly restored both house and gardens.

Decorating the gardens are some pieces of stonework brought by the Stapyltons from the ruins of Byland Abbey, which they owned in the reign of George IV. An altar and a statue were also acquired to enhance the gardens and summer house but later returned. It is even said that one member of the family had the remains of Roger de Mowbray, who founded the Cistercian Abbey in 1177, removed from Byland and carried under the seat of his carriage to be buried in Myton churchyard. Whether or not this is true remains a mystery to this day, but it makes an intriguing story.

NETHER SILTON *Grid ref. SE 459923*

—— Nether Silton lies on the Hambleton Hills, on the edge of the national park, and is reached by a twisting and picturesque road off the A19 to Northallerton. It is a tiny secluded and attractive village, with a little church, whose altar rails are reputed to be made of wood from HMS *Dreadnought* of Nelson's day.

In a field behind the church, from which one has a view across the hills to the plain, stands a solitary rough-hewn stone about five feet in height. It appears at first sight to be just a stone, nothing of any great interest – an old gatepost perhaps – but on closer inspection it bears on one side a mysterious inscription:

HTGOMHS
TBBWOTGWWG
TWOTEWAHH
ATCLABWHEY
AD 1765
AWPSAYAA

It is said to have been carved for Silton's Squire Hickes in the 18th century and to commemorate an old manor house which once stood there, each letter representing a word, as follows:

Here The Grand Old Manor House Stood
The Black Beams Were Oak The Great Walls Were Good
The Walls Of The East Wing Are Hidden Here
A Thatched Cottage Like A Barn Was Here Erected Year
AD 1765
A Wide Porch Spans A Yard And Alcove

A building with mullioned windows nearby may be part of the old house. The mystery remains, however; what became of the old manor and the cottage like a barn, and above all why did the squire choose such an eccentric and enigmatic way of conveying the message?

NORTHALLERTON *Grid ref. SE 371937*

At the narrowest point of the Vale of York, where it is only 10 miles wide, lies Northallerton, once the county town of the North Riding and now, since the local government reorganisation of 1974, the administrative centre of North

Yorkshire. It is also a thriving market town, its broad High Street crammed with market stalls and bustling with shoppers every Wednesday.

In 1069 William the Conqueror sent his soldiers to lay waste the town in revenge and retribution for the death of the Governor of Northumbria, who was killed by Yorkshire peasants in reaction to his cruelty. In the terrible famine that followed, the citizens dying of starvation were reduced to eating the flesh of any animals they could lay their hands on to survive: cats, dogs, rats and even, it is said, human flesh.

An obelisk a few miles out of Northallerton towards Darlington commemorates the Battle of the Standard in August 1138, when the invading Scots were decisively beaten by the English. The battle takes its name from the strange standard composed of a ship's mast mounted on a wagon, with the Host and a cross at the top, and the banners of St Peter of York, St John of Beverley, St Cuthbert of Durham and St Wilfrid of Ripon attached. It is illustrated on the obelisk.

By the early 19th century the town was an important staging post on the routes from London and York to the north, with four coaching inns on the High Street. The Fleece, the oldest building in the town, was much admired by Charles Dickens. The Golden Lion, built in 1700, had many distinguished guests, including the Tsar of Russia. In the Second World War it was the victim of a prank by Canadian airmen from Leeming when they stole its golden lion. But, as is plain to see, it was duly returned. With the arrival of the railway in 1841 the day of the coach was over.

Like Richmond, Northallerton had a Georgian theatre, in the delightfully named Tickle Toby Yard, and like Richmond's (see page 124) it went through many uses – a Methodist chapel, an abattoir and a gymnasium. Unlike Richmond's, it has not been restored and today is the Sportsman's Club. But what sights and sounds it must have known over the years.

The unexpected sight of a vine on the wall of the Rutson Hospital is worth looking out for, although it is but a descendant and a shadow of what once was there. Already 200 years old at the end of the 16th century, it was reputedly the largest in Europe and had a trunk four feet in circumference and branches 100 feet long.

NORTH GRIMSTON *Grid ref. SE 845675*

Just a few houses on the B1248 road from Malton to Beverley, nothing special, one might think; that's North Grimston – a place that people pass through. But, inside the plain and simple little church of St Nicholas, a very old and wonderful treasure is to be seen, which is possibly older than the church itself. It is a heavy tub-like font, said to be Norman, like parts of the church, but the crude but clear carvings covering the entire surface of its straight sides are suggestive of an even earlier period. One half shows the Lord and his Disciples at the Last Supper, with details of fish, bread and goblets all clearly depicted on the table – and their little legs dangling beneath it. On the other side are St Nicholas and the Descent from the Cross. An old-fashioned plough at the back of the church is the parish plough, used in the past to till the church lands and perhaps also loaned out to others in need of it.

North Grimston may be small but it does have something that was once a common feature of many villages and has now

The Last Supper, North Grimston.

become rare. It has a working forge. When horses were used for work on the land and as the only means of transport in both town and country, the blacksmith was an essential member of any community, not only as a farrier shoeing the horses, but also as the maker and repairer of farm implements. Just inside the gateway of the forge here is a curious reddish-brown erection with a textured surface and a crescent shape decorating the top. Set further back is yet another one. Are they perhaps pieces of modern sculpture or strange relics from the past? They could indeed be regarded as both, for, on closer inspection, they prove to be made up of discarded horseshoes, rusted to a lovely rich colour. There are an estimated 65,000 shoes in two columns, which were built, I am told, purely for the sake of tidiness and with no artistic intent. They are certainly a testimony to the past and present work of the farrier in this area; horses are still very much a feature of the countryside, with several racing stables nearby and not far away a farmer who, to the delight of visitors, demonstrates the old ways of farming with horses.

NUNNINGTON *Grid ref. SE 665795*

─── Three parallel roads make up the grey stone village of Nunnington, situated on the ridge known as Caulkley's Bank, which extends from the moors into the Vale of Pickering. One road leads down through an avenue of trees to the 18th century bridge over the River Rye, with Nunnington Hall, built on the site of a nunnery, beside it. The second goes down from the church to the school at the bottom – notice too the ancient almshouses – while the cottages and the Royal Oak Inn on the third road are fronted by high grassy banks. All three are joined by little alleys and yards.

The 17th century hall, owned by the National Trust, makes a charming picture with its gables and mullioned windows and its beautiful setting. It is open to the public from April to October. If visiting there be sure to venture as far as the attics to see the collection of remarkable miniature rooms furnished to scale in period style. In the grounds rare old species of apple trees are cultivated. Like all self-respecting old manor houses, Nunnington has its haunted room. The panelled room first earned its reputation in 1937, when a French visitor slept there and experienced a presence, but the ghost herself is said to come from long before that time and to be that of a grief-stricken mother whose son fell from a window and was killed. The rustle of her silk dress signals her presence as she glides through the room lamenting her loss.

Nor is this the only ghostly happening associated with this lovely spot. The sound of galloping hooves can sometimes be heard in the village at dead of night, since a horse and cart came down the hill too fast one night, crashed into the bridge and fell into the waters of the Rye.

On Rogation Sunday in May an old tradition is carried out by the church congregation when they process around the church, pausing to pray to the north, south, east and west for farmers, fishermen and workers in industry, in each direction.

OLDSTEAD *Grid ref. SE 535805*

When monks from Furness were seeking a place to build their abbey, Stocking – now Oldstead – at the foot of the Hambleton Hills was one of several places that they settled in for a while before finally building it at Byland.

On the hill behind the village is a tall tower rising from above the trees of the Forestry plantation. It was built at the instigation of John Wormald of Oldstead Hall to commemorate the reign of the new monarch, Queen Victoria. Known as Mount Snever Observatory, it housed a large telescope and other astronomical instruments, and gave a view of extraordinary distance across the countryside. There is no access to the tower today, but it can be reached in a pleasant outing for the serious walker, armed with stout shoes and a good map. The building bears several inscriptions, but they are not easy to decipher. Credit is given to the builder and also to John Wormald, and a long poem pays tribute to Queen Victoria and the glories of her reign – presumably largely anticipated, since the tower was erected in her first year on the throne.

Also on the hill, a short distance away, is a little chapel on the site long ago of a battle at Scotch Corner. This is not the Scotch Corner known to travellers going north on the A1. It lies on the old drovers' road, used in the 18th and 19th centuries by drovers from Scotland and the north bringing their cattle and flocks down to markets in the south. At this point the road branched off through Oldstead to the markets in the plain of York, and here in 1322 the Battle of Byland was fought, when Edward II was routed by the Scots; hence the name of the spot.

The little chapel in this isolated place was once a humble farm building, until it was renovated in the 1950s and turned into a chapel of remembrance for all those killed in battle, in particular three former pupils of Ampleforth College, the Roman Catholic public school not far away, who were killed in the Second World War. The carvings on the outside of the building of the Virgin and Child and an angel, and the figure of Christ inside, are the work of John Bunting, a local sculptor. The unusual site and its historic associations give a very special atmosphere to the chapel.

OSMOTHERLEY   *Grid ref. SE 456975*

Like beauty spots everywhere, Osmotherley has a problem with traffic and parked cars. One of the loveliest villages in the North York Moors National Park, it is situated just off the A19 south of Northallerton and is popular with visitors from both southern and northern directions. Not only motorists but walkers too are attracted to the village, which is the starting point for the Lyke Wake Walk across the moors. The 40-mile route to Ravenscar on the east coast, climbing to 5,000 feet over the Cleveland Hills and North York Moors, takes its name from a funeral dirge, the 'Lyke Wake' (meaning 'corpse watch'). The oldest known example of the Yorkshire dialect, it was passed down over the years but not printed until 1686.

It describes the possible journey of the soul through purgatory to hell and the good deeds in life which could ease the suffering, but

> If bite or sup thoo nivver gav nean
> Ivvery neet an' all;
> T' fleames'll bon thee sair ti t'bean
> An' Christ tak up thi sawl.

The walk (which must be completed within 24 hours) was founded by Bill Cowley and first made in October 1955. Since then many hardy spirits have tested their endurance and achieved the distinction of being a successful Lyke Wake walker.

It is quite common for a village to have a market cross and Osmotherley is no exception, but beside it on a small green at the centre of the village is an unusual stone barter table supported on five columns, on which goods to be sold could be displayed and haggled over. John Wesley, known to have been a rather short man, is reputed to have stood on it to preach his sermon in the open air, as was his custom. He visited Osmotherley on several occasions in his travels through Yorkshire and his words seem to have been well taken; up a little alley almost opposite the barter table is the tiny Methodist chapel dated 1754, which must surely be one of the earliest established. A model of simplicity, it is still in use today.

On the edge of the moor, about a mile or so out of Osmotherley on the road to Hawnby, is the old Chequers Inn, standing beside the old drovers' road. This would have been a busy throughfare in the 18th and 19th centuries, with thousands of sheep and cattle driven down from the north to markets in the south. The inn took its name from the tokens issued to the drovers to be exchanged for refreshment as they stopped there on their long and tiring trek. It is no longer an inn but the old inn sign displayed on the outside wall still sounds tempting:

Be not in haste – step in and taste
Ale tomorrow for nothing.

 GREAT OUSEBURN AND LITTLE OUSEBURN *Grid ref. SE 445615*

The two Ouseburn villages – Great Ouseburn and Little Ouseburn – lie very close together and are very similar in appearance, not surprisingly, since they developed as part of the Kirby Hall estate in Victorian times.

If one approaches Little Ouseburn from Aldwark Bridge a sharp eye will notice to the left, just before the gateway and lodge of Kirby Hall, an ice-house, an early form of refrigerator. Ice-houses were common in the heyday of the large country house and were in use from the 18th to the 20th century. Snow and ice were collected in the winter and packed inside these

The source of the Ouse, Ouseburn.

underground chambers, providing ice for use in the kitchens during the summer months. The domed chamber, resembling an igloo constructed of a double layer of bricks with space and straw between, was usually situated on the north side of the house and well covered with earth to provide insulation. The entrance would be blocked with straw. Surprisingly this simple method could often preserve ice for well over a year.

Over a little hump-backed bridge is Holy Trinity church where Anne Brontë worshipped when she was governess for five years to the Robinson family at nearby Thorpe Green. She introduced elements of the area into her novel *Agnes Grey* and made a drawing of the church, which is an ancient one. For a small village church, it has an unusual and striking feature: a large 18th century mausoleum standing close by. It is said to contain 23 bodies, including that of the founder and president of the Royal Agricultural Society, Sir Henry Meysey-Thompson.

Leaving the church at Little Ouseburn and going through Great Ouseburn, an odd protruding stone in the wall by the gate of St Mary's church may catch the eye. It may appear insignificant but it is all that remains of an old preaching cross, where missionaries first preached Christianity. Churches were later usually built on these sites.

A much larger stone marks the source of the River Ouse, though it is not open to immediate view. It stands in a private garden behind the old workhouse, now a seed merchant's store, at the point where the road through the village joins the B6265. It is possible to view it on request. There is actually no sign of water round the 12 feet high pillar, which is surrounded by bushes and flowers, but Ouse Gill Beck, which becomes the Ouse after its junction with the River Ure, rises from a nearby spring.

It is not known when the source stone was erected and it may have been there before the workhouse. A personal feeling, based purely on the visual appearance, is that it could be 18th century. It may once have served as a milestone, as it stands close to the main road, hidden now only by the hedge, and it is inscribed on one side 'Boroughbridge 4 miles', and on the opposite side 'York 13 miles'. To the front it reads 'Ouse River Head', and behind 'Ouse Gill Spring'.

PATELEY BRIDGE *Grid ref. SE 155655*

—— As the crow flies Pateley Bridge is approximately equidistant – a matter of 10 miles or so – from Ripon, Masham and Harrogate. A former quarry and lead mining town on the River Nidd, it is a popular spot today with summer visitors. A plaque on the steep and narrow High Street marks the start and finish of the Nidderdale Way, a circular walk of 53 miles. Less energetic visitors can take a pleasant gentle stroll by the river, or find plenty to interest them in the small town itself, with its varied shops, and the museum housed in the former model workhouse. Look out, too, for the oldest sweet shop in the country.

Above the town, on Guise Cliff, stands the mock ruin known as Yorke's Folly. There are two pillars; a third fell down in 1893. The Yorke family owned nearby Bewerley Hall and gave much to the development of Pateley Bridge. The folly was built by John Yorke to provide work for the unemployed in a period of depression in the latter part of the 18th century. Each worker was provided daily with a loaf of bread and a payment of four old pennies as long as the work lasted. The views from the folly are glorious and worth the climb, but they may well have been of little interest to the workers at the time. It has often been said that 'one can't live off scenery' but today, with many beautiful places depending for their living on tourism, that is surely no longer strictly true.

On the hills nearby is the scenic 80 feet deep How Stean Gorge, where How Stean Beck winds its way through the limestone cliffs; here hanging creepers drip from the rocks and strange ferns grow in abundance. It is a place well suited to the legends of fiends and dreadful bogies that once abounded in the dales.

The road out of Pateley Bridge to Grassington climbs steeply up a great hill to Greenhow, which, situated in bleak countryside 1,300 feet above sea level, is Yorkshire's highest village. Beyond, by the roadside, is Stump Cross Cavern stretching for a thousand yards underground. Hidden and unknown for centuries until discovered by accident by lead miners in 1860, the fantastic underground display of stalagmites and stalactites is in sharp contrast to the bleak and barren countryside above. One can enjoy the wonders of this subterranean world daily from March to September. Hard hats are provided, but be sure to wrap up warmly – no matter how hot overhead, it's jolly cold down there!

PICKERING   *Grid ref. SE 798839*

—— Once a vast lake, formed in the glacial period and three times the size of Windermere, the Vale of Pickering stretches from the Hambleton Hills to the coast. At the approach to the North York Moors and giving its name to the vale is the ancient market town of Pickering.

A motte and bailey castle was built in Norman times on the northern side of the town, and added to in the 14th century. Richard II was imprisoned there in 1399 before being sent to his death in Pontefract. The ruins of the outer walls and towers are extensive and still impressive today.

At the opposite side of the town, the parish church, its tall steeple rising from behind the red-roofed houses, is reached by an alleyway and many steps. The church's great treasures, the exquisite, richly coloured 15th century wall paintings, were once hidden behind whitewash and only uncovered and restored in the late 19th century. A large painting of the traveller's saint, St Christopher, carrying the Christ Child on his shoulders, faces one from the wall opposite the door immediately on entry. Other paintings depict St Edmund riddled by four archers' arrows, St Thomas à Becket's martyrdom, scenes from the life of St Catherine of Alexandria, St John the Baptist and Salome, and many more.

In 1943 the artist Rex Whistler, whose decorative works adorned the walls of such places as the tearooms of the Tate Gallery in London, added his own contribution to mural paintings in the town by painting *The Children eating Cakes* for a children's Christmas party in the Memorial Hall. He was a captain in the army at the time, stationed at the Castle Camp in Pickering, and sadly was killed in Normandy the following year. It is possible that the painting that he did for that Christmas party was one of his last works. Two flat-backed wooden figures of Welsh guardsmen also painted by him can be seen in the Beck Isle Museum.

The museum, which is open daily from the end of March to the end of October, shows bygones of local life and customs and examples of rural crafts. Among the documents and books owned by the museum are the works of William Marshall, the important rural economist and advocate of the need for agricultural colleges. When he died in 1818 he was involved in establishing the very first agricultural college in England, in his own home, which now houses the museum.

We cannot leave Pickering without mention of a surprising connection between this little rural town and the capital of the United States of America. Robert King (1740–1817) and his son Nicholas, natives of Pickering and both surveyors, were leading figures in the planning of the city of Washington DC.

PORT MULGRAVE *Grid ref. NZ 796174*

On the coast between Runswick Bay and Staithes lies a tiny abandoned harbour, unknown to many who visit the area. Like many lost villages it owes its demise to a change in the local industry. The little harbour crumbles quietly away, used only by a few private small boats. It was built in the second half of the 19th century by Charles Palmer of Jarrow, who founded the Grinkle Park Mining Company at the height of the iron-ore mining boom in the district. He was the owner of several blast furnaces in Jarrow and sought to control the process from beginning to end by shipping the ore direct from the mine via the port to his furnaces. The ore was transported from the mine by narrow-gauge railway, and to get it down the steep cliffs to the harbour the trucks were pulled by a stationary engine through a mile-long tunnel. Its exit onto the harbour can still be seen, though it is now bricked up for safety reasons.

The port, so quiet and peaceful now, was a very busy place at its peak, handling as much as 3,000 tons of ore a week. Its closure in the 1920s was brought about by the importation of cheaper ore from abroad – a familiar story in many industries. The magnificent views out to sea remain, however, and make it worth following the road in the village of Hinderwell that leads to the few remaining cliff-top cottages of Port Mulgrave. A gate opposite the cottages gives access to a steep path down the cliff to this small piece of Yorkshire history.

RASKELF *Grid ref. SE 492710*

—— A village of red brick cottages in agricultural countryside, Raskelf lies between the A19 and the main railway line to Scotland, three miles west of the market town of Easingwold. It consists of one long street with a crossroads at its centre and beside the crossroads is the village pound or pinfold, where stray animals used to be impounded. They would be released to their owners on payment of a small fine to the pinder, the man in charge of rounding up the strays. Pounds were once a common feature of the countryside but usually they did not survive for long when no longer in use. Even the more substantially built soon became dilapidated and were demolished. Thankfully that did not happen here, for there can surely have been few strays housed in such imposing style as those at Raskelf.

The pinfold, Raskelf.

Like the village houses, the little building is made of brick. Its pointed arched windows and door, and battlemented top, give it a rather Gothic appearance, although it was built in the 18th century. It was restored to its present state in 1971.

At the end of the village street is St Mary's, a church which has an unusual feature making it unique in the whole of Yorkshire. The square 15th century tower is built entirely of attractively weathered timber, from its pyramid shaped top down to the ground. Another unusual feature is the rare timber arcade leading into the north chapel.

Inside this quaint church is a tribute to a brave man, Augustus Cavendish Webb, who died leading his men in the infamous Charge of the Light Brigade – a far cry from the quiet little village of Raskelf to the noise and slaughter of war in the Crimea.

REETH   *Grid ref. SE 037991*

Reeth is described by some as the 'capital of Swaledale', and certainly it is the largest village in the dale. Its grey houses and numerous old inns – one, the King's Arms, bears a datestone of 1734 – cluster around the large central green on the sunny lower slope of Calva Hill, overlooking the plain of the River Swale and its tributary Arkle Beck, with the dramatic fells as backdrop.

In Anvil Square the rounded corner of the pottery building, once a blacksmith's shop, is noteworthy. It was designed as a safety measure against harm to livestock and horses. The door of the building has 'hornburns' on it – initials branded on the horns of sheep as a means of identification. Stone is to be seen all around – stone roofs are a feature – showing the use of local materials. Note too the stone-pillared water pumps, which provided an important source of water before plumbing was installed in the houses. Reeth Bridge, a stone bridge with safety recesses for pedestrians, was the work of John Carr of York in the 18th century.

Farming, mainly of sheep and cattle, has long been a way of life in Swaledale, giving it the typical landscape of stone walls and field barns in the meadows and pastures below the fells. Today tourism is an important addition to farming, but in the past Reeth was a centre of the lead mining industry, the various techniques of which have also left their mark on the landscape.

The earliest of these was the method known as 'hushing'; this entailed creating a dam of water, which was then allowed to rush in a torrent down the hillside to remove the subsoil and thus expose the ore, leaving as a consequence areas of bare rock. Later, tunnels were made into the rock to reach the ore, the entrances to these disused mines presenting a danger today to the unwary or foolhardy on the hills. Most dangerous of all, however, are the shafts which were dropped from the moor tops. But while the dangers today are avoidable, those old miners faced danger and hardship in the mines every day of their working lives. The peak of the Swaledale mining industry was in the 200 years up to 1870; thereafter the arrival of cheap ore from such places as Spain meant that it was unable to compete. At one time as many as 4,000 men were producing 40,000 tons of lead a year. Workers had arrived from other parts of the country for the mining, from as far away as Cornwall and Wales, but with the decline of the industry came a dramatic drop in the local population as miners left with their families to find work in the Durham coalfields or the Lancashire cotton mills, or even to emigrate to foreign fields.

RICHMOND   *Grid ref. NZ 175009*

It has been called the 'Heart of the Dales', or the 'Gateway to Swaledale', and its name means 'strong hill' from Old French *riche monte*. It was quite probably the site's commanding position that influenced the Norman, Alan of Brittany, later Earl of Richmond, when he built his massive castle here. From the height of the cliff overlooking the River Swale, the impregnable fortress commanded the entrance to the dale. Unlike others at the time, it was built in stone from the start. Today, the castle, now in the care of English Heritage, still dominates the town which grew up around it.

Undoubtedly one of the most romantic towns in the county, Richmond was almost completely rebuilt in the 18th century, and there is still a Georgian air about the place, despite the modern elements that have since been introduced, especially around the large cobbled market square. At the bottom of the sloping square, Holy Trinity church (now a regimental museum) had shops built into its walls, and has been described by Pevsner as 'the queerest ecclesiastical building one can imagine'. When it was undergoing conversion for use as the museum, a lead box containing documents and memorabilia of the eclipse of 1927 was found embedded in the walls.

Richmond's greatest treasure from the Georgian period is the little theatre, tucked away beside a public house, which is said to be the oldest surviving professional theatre in its original condition. Samuel Butler (1750–1812) was its originator, and he formed a touring company that covered an area from Whitby to Northallerton. He opened his theatre in Richmond in 1788, but after it closed in 1830 it suffered the indignity of a variety of uses, including becoming an auction room and a furniture warehouse. After restoration, it was reopened in May 1963 by the Princess Royal. Miraculously many of the original features had been found intact – including the 'kicking boards', used to express disapproval. Their use must have been very satisfying to the patrons, but not, I imagine, to the actors.

The architect John Carr of York built Green Bridge, which crosses the Swale to Richmond Green. In the middle are carved the names of the mayors 1788–9. Another name to look for is that

Richmond Castle.

of John Wycliffe the reformist clergyman, born in 1325, who instituted the first translation of the Bible from Latin into English, in the belief that all should be able to understand it for themselves. Back in the market place look for the plaque on the Yorkshire Building Society; though he was not born in Richmond, but in nearby Hipswell, this commemoration of him is placed here, where it is likely to be seen by more people.

Frances I'Anson, the 'sweet lass of Richmond Hill' of musical renown, was also not born in the town (see page 92), but has associations with Hill House in Richmond through her maternal grandparents.

![] RIPLEY *Grid ref. SE 284605*

—— A stranger arriving in Ripley might well be bemused, thinking him or herself in France rather than in Nidderdale, Yorkshire, and with good reason, for in the early 1800s this attractive estate village near Harrogate was entirely rebuilt by Sir William Ingilby of Ripley Castle, in the style of a village he had seen in Alsace-Lorraine. The village hall bears the inscription *Hotel de Ville*. Sir William obviously had a taste for things Continental, as he called his castle *Das Schloss* and a sign at the entrance commands *Parlez au Suisse*. It is all somewhat confusing to find in Yorkshire, but visitors speaking only English are still welcome. Ripley Castle has been the home of the Ingilbys since 1345 and the present owner opens his historic home and beautiful gardens to the general public on a regular basis.

There is a story that Oliver Cromwell spent a night at the castle after the Battle of Marston Moor, while Sir William Ingilby and his sister Jane, who dressed and fought like a man, and was always known as Trooper Jane, were still away fighting for the King. Cromwell was denied a comfortable bed and was watched over the entire night by Lady Ingilby with a pair of pistols to hand. She is said to have remarked afterwards that it was as well that he had behaved well, or he would not have left alive. Another version of the story is that Trooper Jane and her brother had returned from the battle and that, while Sir William hid in a priest hole in the castle, it was his sister Jane, who, though wounded, was the one that might have changed the course of English history had Cromwell not conducted himself well.

Certainly in 1963 a secret hiding place was discovered behind panelling in the Knight's Chamber in the castle. It may have been used by Francis Ingilby, who was ordained as a Catholic priest in 1583 and was eventually put to death in York for his religion.

Cromwell is also said to have stabled his horses in the ancient parish church of All Saints, and hollows in the stones of the east wall are claimed to be bullet holes, caused when Royalists were lined up and shot. It has been pointed out that the holes are very high, suggesting that the firing squad were not very good shots and missed their targets quite a few times.

In the churchyard is a curious object known as a weeping cross. The purpose of such crosses, which are sited in churchyards or on the route followed by funeral cortèges, is not entirely clear. It is believed that the niches around the base supported the kneeling weepers at a funeral as they prayed for the redemption of the sins of themselves and the deceased. However, it has also been suggested that they were in fact for votive offerings from the mourners, and the eight niches at Ripley do seem rather narrow for an adult to kneel in.

RIPON   *Grid ref. SE 318709*

—— 'As true as Ripon steel' is an old saying reminding us of the fact that Ripon was once famous for its steel rowels (the spiked wheel once found on spurs), the best in the world. It was said that the spikes could pierce a shilling piece without bending or blunting. This explains the steel rowel's incorporation into the coat of arms of this small historic city.

The streets of Ripon, many of them called 'gates' as they are in York, are full of character and interest with old coaching inns and Georgian buildings, but the city was founded long before that time, and the interiors of these buildings behind their Georgian facades are in many cases from very much earlier periods. The old wakeman's house at one end of the market square proclaims its great age openly. The large, almost square market place at the centre of the city is the scene every night of an ancient custom, more than 1,000 years old, known as 'setting the watch'. At nine o'clock the hornblower or wakeman, dressed in traditional garb with a tricorne hat, blows a curved silver-bound horn to mark the curfew, first at the 90 feet high obelisk in the square, which replaced an older one, and then before the town hall. In medieval times this was the hour at which all fires were to be extinguished. The wakeman in the Middle Ages was a figure somewhat similar to our present day mayor, and with his constables he was responsible for the safety of the citizens and their property, for which 2d was paid for each door by the householder as a kind of insurance. The words of the city motto 'Except Ye Lord Keep Ye Cittie Ye Wakeman Waketh In Vain' cannot be missed, beautifully inscribed across the front of the town hall. When elected by the Aldermen of the city, should the wakeman refuse to serve, he faced a very heavy fine, a fact which has given a tradition today of 'seeking the mayor' – a sort of hide-and-seek game acted out prior to the mayor's taking up office!

Once a year, a citizen in the guise of St Wilfrid, the patron saint of Ripon, processes through the streets of the city, mounted on a white horse. St Wilfrid is also associated with the cathedral, one of the smallest in the country. All periods of architecture are represented in the cathedral but the Saxon crypt, built by St Wilfrid and dating back more than 1,000 years, is a very rare feature. This fascinating narrow stone cell, which has survived while the church above it has been destroyed and rebuilt over the centuries, contains a narrow opening in one wall known as St Wilfrid's Needle. It is said that anyone who can squeeze through it is sure of forgiveness although according to an older tradition the ability to do so was a sign of chastity. There are many interesting monuments and tablets in the cathedral. Look out for the bust of Hugh Ripley, the last wakeman and first mayor; the inscription to William Finney, who was 103 when he died; Admiral Oxley with his wife and seven cherubic children; and John Elliot, who sailed the world with Captain Cook.

But above all do not miss seeing the wonderful and often amusing carvings on the undersides of the misericords in the choir. These enabled old or weak monks to rest on the tipped-up seats while giving the impression of standing during Divine Office. The name derives from Latin *misericordia* 'pity.' Although the names of the carvers of misericords are usually unknown, Ripon is fortunate in having records to show that its carvings, dating from 1489 to 1494, were the work of a group led by William Bromflet, which had great influence throughout the north of England. As we have already seen (page 80), it was the inspiration of Robert Thompson of Kilburn.

The subjects of the carvings were often taken from contemporary prints and Old Testament scenes from the woodblock book *Biblia Pauperum*. Religious subjects are rare on misericords and Old Testament scenes not often seen elsewhere. The most popular subjects are incidents from everyday life, fables, proverbs, seasons and strange beasts. These scenes may nevertheless have moral and Christian implications. Look, for example, for a man wheeling in a barrow a woman with a bottle in her hand, Samson carrying the gates of Gaza, Caleb and Joshua bearing grapes from the Promised Land (supported by strange figures called Blemya, whose faces are in their stomachs) and a fox in a pulpit preaching to a goose.

Also not to be missed is a rich and intricate carving on the end of the bishop's bench in the choir. It shows an elephant with a castle on its back and a man clutched in its trunk. It is standing on a turtle and below is a centaur holding a shield – just one of the intriguing items in this choir of wonderful carvings.

ROBIN HOOD'S BAY   *Grid ref. NZ 955055*

Although parts of Yorkshire do lay claim to connections with the legendary Robin Hood, there is no evidence of any such connection here. The name Robin Hood's Bay was first applied to the town in the reign of Henry VIII, but it is always called Bay Town by the locals. The main street descends so steeply down to the bay that the pavement alongside it is a flight of steps, indeed the whole of the old town tumbles higgledy-piggledy down the cliff in a veritable warren of cobbled streets, alleys and steps. The houses, built one above the other, are said to contain secret passages and hidden cupboards, a relic of the town's past history as a hotbed of smuggling, when it was said that men and goods could be passed from one end of the town to the other, without ever appearing in the open. One alley, serving perhaps as an escape route, not only from the customs men, but also from that other scourge, the press-gang, is named The Bolts.

Look out for a particular feature of the houses, with an unusual purpose – the 'coffin windows' – so called because the staircases are so narrow and twisting that the little windows are needed on the landings, specifically to enable coffins unable to negotiate the bends to be lowered through them to the street below. The best-known example is in Littlewood Cottage, which can be reached by turning left from the dock, up Tyson's Steps, then left again after 'Sunnyside'. Notice too, down towards the dock, the plaque marking the house where the late, once popular author Leo Walmsley lived. His books featured Robin Hood's Bay under the name of Bramblewick, and at least one, *Sea Fever*, was made into a film.

Today Robin Hood's Bay depends largely on tourism, and many of its quaint cottages are now holiday homes. In the past, smuggling apart, its main business was the equally hazardous one of fishing, with the inevitable tragedies and heroic deeds that go with it. Numerous ships have been wrecked in the bay. In a storm in 1893 the bowsprit of a ship named *The Romulus* was driven right through the window of the Bay Hotel. The most famous rescue in the bay was in 1881, when the Whitby lifeboat, unable to be launched there because of high seas, was manhandled overland in waist high snowdrifts to Robin Hood's Bay to save the six-man crew of a brig named *Visitor*. The rescue was led by the famous Henry Freeman, the only survivor of the Whitby lifeboat crew in an incident in 1861; he was the only member of the crew wearing the new cork life-jacket when the boat was overwhelmed. When Freeman retired as coxswain in 1899, he had helped to save 300 lives along this coast.

Over the years, as many as 200 houses have been lost to the sea, due to the erosion of the cliffs. The protective seawall built in 1974 gives the added attraction of a promenade for the visitors to this popular spot, sometimes known as the 'Yorkshire Clovelly'.

ROSEDALE ABBEY *Grid ref. SE 726959*

Rosedale is a beautiful valley in the North York Moors, about nine miles long, with the River Seven and a road running through it, and at its centre is the village of Rosedale Abbey. The second half of the village's name refers to the Cistercian nunnery founded there in the 11th or 12th century. It is a slight misnomer, however, as St Mary's was a priory and not an abbey. All that remains of it are a few stones, a spiral stone staircase and a stone inscribed with the words *omnia vanitas*, Latin for 'all is vanity', which has been incorporated above the door of the parish church.

Stones from the priory were taken to build houses in 1850 for the miners who flocked there with the boom in ironstone extraction. Ironstone had been mined in the region as early as the monastic times, and old tracks radiating from Rosedale Abbey were once used by miners riding their donkeys to and from the ironstone works thereabouts. Ironstone is magnetic and often drew the lightning; when it did, in those more superstitious times, it is said that the villagers thought that the Devil lurked there in the hills. In the 19th century, at the height of the industry, three mines worked the rich deposits, and the population grew to as many as 3,000. A railway was built across the moor top, connecting Rosedale with Teeside, but by 1926 the last mine had closed, and soon after that the railway was taken up, leaving only reminders in the dale of its industrial past. The disused pits remain, as well as a row of kilns. Rosedale chimney, 100 feet high, was a landmark for miles around until 1972, when it became unsafe and was demolished. It stood on Bank Top, a one-in-three hill, whose steepness caused it also to be familiarly called Rosedale Chimney.

Many of the cottages have now been turned into holiday homes and nature has softened any industrial scars, so that Rosedale's industrial history might almost never have been.

RUNSWICK BAY *Grid ref. NZ 808161*

—— In 1901 the women of Runswick Bay manned the lifeboat and went to the rescue of their menfolk, caught in their fishing cobles by a sudden squall. They were a hardy lot, as indeed they needed to be; life for the fishermen and their families on this picturesque coast was harsh and hazardous. When the sea claimed its victims, as it all too frequently did, and eventually gave them up, often the only means of identification was the knitted guernsey worn by the fishermen, each village having its own distinctive pattern for that very purpose.

The village lies to one side of the wide sandy bay, approached by a narrow precipitous road. The little cottages with their red pantiled roofs – many of them now holiday cottages – seem to tumble down the cliff face to the sea. In 1682, in a great landslip, the entire village, apart from a single house, did exactly that! Had it not been for mourners returning late from a funeral wake nearby, who, realising what was happening, were able to warn them, all the villagers too might have perished along with their homes. The village was rebuilt, but the unstable cliffs and continual coastal erosion eventually necessitated the building of a protective seawall in 1970, to prevent any repeat of history.

On the far side of the bay is Hob Hole, a cave said to be inhabited by a hob (a goblin) with the power to cure the 'kincough' (whooping cough). All that was needed was to approach the cave and recite the magic words, 'Hob! Hob! Ma bairn's getten t'kincough. Tak it off! Tak it off!' Did it work? Well, some children did recover from whooping cough!

SALTERSGATE   *Grid ref. SE 855945*

Not far from the Hole of Horcum and the stretch of road known as the Devil's Elbow, on the road that crosses the moors from Pickering to Whitby, is the Saltersgate Inn, where the fire, originally of peat, has been kept burning continuously since around 1800. It is said that if the fire were ever to be allowed to go out, the ghost of an exciseman who was murdered there will return to haunt the place.

The inn was once a centre for the smuggling of salt from Whitby along the route known as the Salt Road or the Old Fish Road. Until 1825 salt was very heavily taxed, resulting in a massive smuggling trade, particularly between 1798 and 1805, when the tax was at its most excessive. This solitary – and in those days remote – inn on the moors was an ideal spot for the smuggled salt to be stored and for fishermen to salt their fish before transporting it inland for sale. It is possible that originally the fire was kept burning simply to make sure that the salt stored there did not become damp. Or was it, as the legend says, to prevent the discovery of a body hidden beneath it? In 1800 a lone exciseman, spying out the activity at the inn, was set upon and killed by a number of smugglers. A new fireplace was installed in the inn soon afterwards and the story arose that the body, which was never found, lay buried underneath it.

Visitors to the inn today can see the old-fashioned black iron fireplace, with the fire still burning in the grate, and ask themselves whether it does indeed hide that old murder victim. And would his ghost really appear should the fire go out? No one knows, but no one is taking the risk! The tradition goes on.

SCARBOROUGH *Grid ref. TA 039887*

———— Known as the 'Queen of Watering Places', Scarborough is England's oldest seaside resort. In 1626 a Mrs Farrow discovered a mineral spring in the cliffs of South Bay, and by 1660 Scarborough had gained a national reputation as a spa. It was the first place to promote sea bathing as beneficial to health, as recommended by Dr Robert Wittie of York. The men bathed naked from boats a little way out to sea, the women in voluminous costumes from bathing machines at the water's edge.

Over the years the town has gained many interesting and distinguished buildings. One such is the Rotunda Museum, built in 1829 by Scarborough Philosophical Society to house the collection of William Smith (1769–1839) of Scarborough, who is regarded as the father of English geology. He identified the age of different rock strata by means of the characteristic groups of fossils they contained. The circular plan and layout of the museum was Smith's own design, displaying the exhibits in layers from floor to ceiling to show the periods in an easy-to-understand fashion. He also installed a unique viewing platform on wheels, from which they could be studied. Though no longer working, it is still to be seen in the museum, which is now largely given over to archaeological displays.

Above the museum is the Grand Hotel, originally associated with the Laughton family, of which the actor Charles Laughton was a member. It is 13 storeys high on the seaward side, and its unusual domed architectural features have caused it to be likened to a sow turned upside down!

At the far end of South Bay, overlooking the harbour, and tucked away down a little alley, is the Three Mariners, said to be 600 years old and one of the earliest public houses in the town, though it is no longer an inn. Once connected with smuggling, it has also served as a small maritime museum and, with its proximity to the harbour, it has also been used in the past as a mortuary for the bodies of sailors brought ashore after disasters at sea.

Almost next door is the 14th century house known as Richard III's House, where Richard is said to have lodged. Built of stone, with a gabled end and mullioned windows, it is all that remains of a larger house.

The castle, built by the Normans, looms over the old town from the cliff above, and high on Castle Hill is St Mary's church, where Anne Brontë, the youngest of the Brontë sisters, is buried.

Three Mariners, Scarborough.

She loved Scarborough and came with her sister Charlotte in 1849. She was desperately ill with consumption, and it was hoped that the sea air would do her good, but she died within days of her arrival. She was just 28 years old.

Her grave, with flowers growing on it, is in the part of the graveyard which is separate from the church. It can be approached by the steep steps behind the Three Mariners – a stiff climb but affording some wonderful views over the town and sea – or by the longer route through the centre of the old town. If you take the latter route, be sure to look out for the old butter cross in Princess Square.

SCORTON   *Grid ref. NZ 255005*

The large central green in the village of Scorton is raised some 3 feet above the level of the road and reached by steps at intervals along its edges. It is one of only two places in the country with an elevated green. Teams of both men and women play cricket on it. But it is the sport of archery for which Scorton has been famed since 1673, when the annual contest for the Scorton Silver Arrow was first played. The silver arrow is thought to have been presented as an archery trophy by Queen Elizabeth I to the Oxford colleges. It was won on one occasion by John Wastell from Scorton, who brought it back to the village and kept it, instead of returning it as he should. John, who was a rather disreputable character, was finally thrown out by his family, and the silver arrow lay forgotten in the attic of the manor house until it was eventually discovered and the competition for it was set up.

An ancient rule of the Scorton Archery Society stated that if any member 'shall that day curse or swear in the hearing of any of the company he shall forthwith pay down one shilling, and so proportionately for every oath, to be distributed by the Captain to the use of the poor of that place or township where they shoot'. Poor shots and lack of restraint must have been the secret hopes of the day of those in need!

Originally only a Yorkshireman could win the arrow, but today anyone is eligible. It goes to the first archer who hits a 3-inch black disc in the centre of the gold at a distance of 100 yards. The holder of the arrow then becomes the captain of the society for the following year and chooses the next venue, which must be in Yorkshire. Other awards apart from the coveted silver arrow include the booby prize of a horn spoon, which may be almost as old as the arrow. The historic trophies, archives and memorabilia are to be displayed in the future at the Royal Armouries in Leeds.

It is interesting that Roger Ascham, the writer of a classic work on archery, was born only a few miles away, at Kirby Wiske, in 1515. Indeed, as tutor in archery to Elizabeth I, he may have had some connection to the Scorton Silver Arrow, believed to be the oldest sporting trophy in England.

SELBY *Grid ref. SE 615325*

How many provincial towns can claim as Selby does the distinction of being the birthplace of a king of England? Henry, the younger son of William the Conqueror, who became Henry I in 1100 after the death of his older brother William Rufus, is traditionally said to have been born here. He can be seen in the stained glass of the south window of Selby Abbey, lying in his cradle and watched over by his mother Matilda, while her ladies-in-waiting work on the Bayeux Tapestry.

Queen Victoria and Prince Albert are also represented in a window of the abbey, and the figures of King George V and Queen Mary are easily recognisable in the niches of the buttresses on either side of the west door. In addition, George V is to be found inside the abbey, in a very unusual place; a tiny bust of him is hidden away inside a leafy but hollow capital in the arcading above the stone seats in the north choir aisle. If you want to see him, be sure to take a torch to help you peer between the leaves!

In 1969 the 900-year-old abbey was chosen as the venue for the distribution by our present Queen, of the Royal Maundy money. Originally a ceremony in which the feet of the poor were washed to commemorate Christ's washing of the disciples' feet, it has long been replaced by the giving of specially minted silver coins on Maundy Thursday, the day before Good Friday, to the same number of recipients as the years of the monarch's age.

But it is not only royalty who have their connections with the abbey. A shield in a window in the south clerestory of the sacristy shows the coat of arms of the Washington family. With its three red stars and two stripes, it was the inspiration for George Washington, the first President of the United States of America, for the flag popularly known as the Stars and Stripes.

The town grew up around the Benedictine abbey, the first monastery to be founded in the north after the Conquest but largely destroyed during the Dissolution of the Monasteries. What remains of it has provided the town with a parish church which is surely one of the most superb in the country, and deserves a book of its own.

Selby is situated on the banks of the River Ouse, less than 10 miles south of York. The only means of crossing the river was by ferry, until 1792, when a wooden trestle bridge was built. The town as we see it today was built largely in the 19th century and developed from a market town to a busy inland port, with flour and oil-cake milling and a thriving shipbuilding industry.

Eventually the bridge that had been a boon became a problem. Though the shipbuilding began to decline, the road traffic grew, and delays at the bridge for the collection of tolls, or the opening of the bridge to allow ships to pass, caused huge tailbacks. In 1991 tolls were abandoned, and today Selby's traffic problems are merely the same as in any other busy town.

SETTLE *Grid ref. SD 815635*

Lying in the valley of the River Ribble, under the towering limestone scar of Castlebergh Crag, Settle, despite the restful sound of its name, was once a busy market town, with cotton mills and tanyards. Today the industry is gone, but the town is still busy as a centre for walkers, cyclists, cavers and visitors of all kinds, many of them drawn to the area of potholes and caves that stretch to the north-west.

An interesting feature of the town itself is the ancient Shambles in the market place, with its six round arches and Victorian houses built above. Nearby is an unusual 17th century house, The Folly, so called because Thomas Preston, who built it, ran out of money and had to leave it unfinished. The Naked Man Café, with its old wall plaque, is well known, but look at it carefully and you will see that the man is not in fact naked, but is wearing a buttoned tunic and knee breeches. He is holding what seems to be a carpenter's plane in front of him, which suggests that this was a 17th century carpenter's or undertaker's sign. His female counterpart can be seen a mile away at Cross Green in Langcliffe. Langcliffe had a Naked Woman inn, now no more, but the stone figure, with a date of 1660 on it, can be seen high on the side of a house. She too is not entirely naked.

Settle can take pride in being the birthplace of Dr George Birkbeck (1776–1841), physician, philanthropist and philosopher. He founded the Mechanics' Institutes, aimed at the education of the workers and dedicated to 'self-improvement and self-help'. More than a hundred were established in Yorkshire alone in the 19th century and others were set up throughout the country. In 1804 Dr Birkbeck settled in London, where he founded the first London Mechanics' Institute in 1823. In 1907 this became

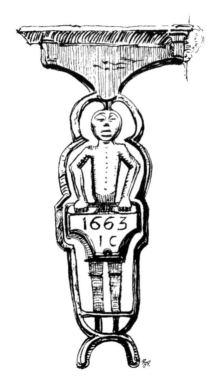

The naked man, Settle.

Birkbeck College, named in his honour, and, in 1920, became part of London University.

SHAROW   *Grid ref. SE 326719*

To the north-east of Ripon, off the A61, is the village of Sharow. Most of the village developed in the 1800s, when the hall was built, together with cottages to accommodate the various workers, gamekeeper, gardeners and others deemed essential to the life of those in the 'big house' at that time. One or two houses are older, having features dating from the 16th and 17th centuries, and modern housing from the 1970s has extended the village considerably from its original size.

St John's church at Sharow was built after the Battle of Waterloo, from a fund set up at that time to build churches throughout England in areas that were without. To the left of the main gate, by the hedge in the churchyard, is a very plain – some might think ugly – monument in the form of a squat grey stone pyramid with a cross atop. It commemorates Charles Piazzi Smyth and his wife Jessie, his 'friend and companion through forty years', who predeceased him, in 1896. Born in Naples in 1819, the son of an admiral, Charles's middle name echoes that of the Italian astronomer Guiseppe Piazzi (1746–1826) and is entirely appropriate for the man who was to become Astronomer Royal for Scotland for 43 years (1845–1888). He was a professor at Edinburgh University, with many astronomical works to his name. The one o'clock time gun, still heard today at Edinburgh Castle, was one of his numerous inventions, and as a skilled photographer he was one of the first to use flash.

With his wife as an enthusiastic assistant, he went to Egypt to study the Pyramids, which he believed held divine guidance for mankind. There they actually lived for some months inside one of the tombs. He was fascinated by the Great Pyramid of Cheops at Giza, which he measured and on which his own monument is based. Though renowned for his travels to many distant places in furtherance of astronomical and scientific objectives, his fanatical interest in the Pyramids and mystical beliefs about them lost him credibility with the authorities.

In 1888 he retired and left Edinburgh for a country house at Ripon. After a long life of journeying, exploration and achievements, he died in 1900, to lie almost forgotten in this quiet country churchyard in Yorkshire.

SHERIFF HUTTON *Grid ref. SE 655665*

Sheriff Hutton, to the south-west of Malton, was one of the villages in the ancient Forest of Galtres, the forest that features in Shakespeare's *Henry IV*. Originally just plain Hutton, it gained its distinctive affix from Bertram de Bulmer, who had his castle here and was made Sheriff of Yorkshire by King Stephen in 1139. This quiet, attractive village, with a sloping green edged by cottages on three sides, and the ruined castle rising above it on its high mound, is steeped in history and atmosphere. The castle passed through marriage to the Neville family, and John Neville rebuilt it in the 14th century into one of the most impressive in the north. Today its six-feet thick walls and four towers are in ruins, except for one of the towers, which is 100 feet high and a landmark for miles around. In the reign of James I, Sir Arthur Ingram was reprimanded many times by the head keeper of Galtres Forest, for taking pieces of the fabric from the castle to build his hunting lodge, the big house nearby known as Sheriff Hutton Park, which is now a school of drama.

Antony Woodville, the brother of Edward IV's queen, spent some time here. A religious man and scholar, he brought back to Sheriff Hutton a French copy of the Latin *Sayings of Philosophers* from one of his pilgrimages. He translated it for Caxton and it became the first dated book (1477) to be printed in England. As a woman, I would like to believe the story that he refused to translate certain derogatory remarks in the book about women and left it to Caxton to do so. He was beheaded by Richard III, with whom the castle at Sheriff Hutton is very much associated. Edward, Earl of Warwick was imprisoned here by Richard and so was Elizabeth of York, whom he hoped to marry after his wife Anne died.

An alabaster monument in a chapel of the church of St Helen and the Holy Cross is generally accepted as that of Edward, Prince of Wales, the son of Richard III and Anne, the daughter of Warwick the Kingmaker, to whom the castle at Sheriff Hutton belonged. The prince is known to have died in Yorkshire, at

Middleham Castle, in 1484, aged about 11. His parents were not in Yorkshire at the time but returned at once for his burial. There is no actual record of its having taken place at Sheriff Hutton and there is no inscription on the monument, but the figure on the tomb is plainly a young boy of noble birth. He is dressed in a long coat called a houpland, with a coronet on his head, which rests on a pillow with griffins or similar winged beasts. Altogether there seems little doubt that this must be the tomb of the young Prince Edward, and great efforts have been made over the years by the Richard III Society to repair the damage caused by age and damp and to continue to preserve it.

SINNINGTON   *Grid ref. SE 744858*

——— This pleasant spot lying off the main road between Pickering and Helmsley has all the requisite features of an English village: cottages with gardens full of bright flowers; a stream crossed by a picturesque 18th century bridge; an ancient church and a tithe barn; a village school set on the broad village green; and a maypole with a fox atop in recognition of the local hunt, which is reputed to be one of the oldest in the country. But Sinnington has a mystery that has puzzled people for centuries.

On the green is a tiny low arched bridge spanning nothing but green grass! Over the years no one has been able to offer an explanation for its presence, though many suggestions have been made. Perhaps the stream once ran on a different course, or a flood channel may have been cut from the stream. Nothing seems to quite fit the bill, and its original purpose remains an enigma still. Whatever it may have been, the tiny, almost fairy-tale bridge, left in isolation on the village green, is a delight.

SKIPTON   *Grid ref. SD 990516*

——— 'Capital of Craven' and 'Gateway to the Dales' are both titles to which the town of Skipton lays claim, and, situated in the Aire Gap, just outside the national park, with the Craven dales to the north and moors to the south, its claims are well justified. Its outstanding feature, the broad tree-lined High Street, bounded by cobbles at each side, is a scene of colourful market stalls on four days of the week, and a big attraction for visitors. At one time the cattle market was held there, until the townspeople decided they had had enough of animals roaming loose along the street, with the smells, dirt and noise, and the farm workers making the most of their day in town. Today's markets are more decorous, though full of bustle, and visitors still make the most of their time in the town.

There are several interesting plaques to look out for along the street, marking the site of the bullring, the pillory and the stocks. Also, at the southern end of the High Street, a plaque referring to Caroline Square indicates that the estranged and ill-used wife of George IV had the support and sympathy of the citizens of Skipton. And how many people, I wonder, know that Thomas Spencer, co-founder of the Marks and Spencer stores, was born in this part of the town? The Craven Museum housed in the Palladian-style town hall is full of local interest, including relics of the former lead mining industry in the dales. Branching off from the High Street, there are interesting little courts and ginnels (alleys) to explore.

The Leeds-Liverpool canal of 1770 runs through the town. This brought industry in textiles to Skipton. Once upon a time, not too far in the past, anyone who had ever so much as sewn on a button was familiar with the word Sylko, the name of the mercerised cotton thread, produced here by Dewhurst's in the mill that dominates the west of the town. Today the canal is given over to pleasure boats and the mills have been taken over by other businesses or converted into flats.

At the northern end of the High Street are the parish church and the castle, which is open to the public for a charge. The castle was built in Norman times by Robert de Romille, but only one gateway remains from this period. In 1309 it passed to the powerful Clifford family and in 1648 it was one of the castles to be destroyed by an order of Parliament for having supported the King in the Civil War. However, it was rebuilt by that indefatigable builder Lady Anne Clifford, whom we have already met at Beamsley. Besides Lady Anne, two members of the Clifford family are notable. One, known as the Sailor Earl, sought danger and adventure with Sir Walter Raleigh on the Spanish Main. He fought the Armada and traditionally it was he who told Elizabeth I of its defeat. When she dropped her glove in excitement at the news, Clifford picked it up and she graciously presented it to him. A miniature in the National Portrait Gallery shows the gallant earl wearing the bejewelled glove in his hat.

Henry Clifford is portrayed as the Shepherd Lord in William Wordsworth's poem *Song at the Feast of Brougham Castle*. He was the son of 'Butcher' Clifford who died in the War of the Roses fighting on the Lancastrian side. Henry, aged seven, was hidden from the vengeance of the King and brought up as a peasant in the home of a shepherd. When, many years later, Henry of Lancaster came to the throne Clifford was able to claim his inheritance and the castle at Skipton, but he still enjoyed the simple life.

On approaching the formidable towered gateway of the castle, one is greeted by the Clifford motto *Desormais* ('henceforth'), carved on the parapet in huge letters of stone. Inside are many delights, as well as a horrible dungeon without light and with little air; it was built below the waterline of the moat to prevent attempts to escape! The Conduit Court, the lovely inner courtyard with the ancient yew tree planted at its centre by Lady Anne Clifford, is a delightful surprise after the heavy outward appearance of the gateway. It is not difficult to imagine the ladies of the Clifford family perhaps strolling and gossiping in this place of tranquillity and beauty.

SLEIGHTS *Grid ref. NZ 865075*

The road from Pickering to Whitby drops down steeply at Blue Bank – so named from the blue lias shale on Sleights Moor – to the village of Sleights and the River Esk. Near Sleights are the remains of an ancient chapel, where, according to legend, an Eskdale hermit was murdered by huntsmen, on the lands of the Abbot of Whitby. As he lay dying, the monk is said to have forgiven his killers, on condition that once a year, on Ascension Eve, they and their descendants, in perpetuity and on pain of losing their estates, plant into the Esk at Whitby a woven fence capable of withstanding three tides. This strange custom, known as Planting the Penny (or Penance) Hedge, is still ceremoniously carried out to this day, though the legend tends to be discounted. It is believed more likely that it is connected with the marking of some ancient boundary.

Passing through Sleights toward the junction with the A171 Whitby to Guisborough road, keep a sharp look out to the left for a sign for Featherbed Lane. Often claimed to be the narrowest highway in England, this stone-paved way, with the inexplicable name, is only about 3 or 4 feet wide. It is an old stone 'trod', a dry route, from the time when packhorses were used to carry goods between villages.

Carry on further along the road, and at the road junction itself a squat stone pillar bears a plaque commemorating an event from World War II. It marks the spot where, on 3rd February 1940, the first enemy aircraft of the war to be shot down crashed into a row of sycamores. The Heinkel bomber was engaged off the coast, by a Hurricane fighter from RAF Acklington. The crippled plane was pursued inland, its rear gunner, despite serious wounds, returning fire the whole way. The pilot of the Hurricane was Group Captain Peter Townsend, who was later to become known for his romance with Princess Margaret. Karl Missy, the German rear gunner, had to have one of his legs amputated in Whitby hospital, where he was visited by Group Captain Townsend. The two airmen also met up with each other once again, much later, in Germany after the war – brave enemies, respecting each other, and emphasising the stupidity of war.

SOUTH KILVINGTON *Grid ref. SE 425845*

The rector of St Wilfrid's church at South Kilvington, just north of Thirsk, in the 19th and early 20th century, was the Rev William Towler Kingsley. A great joker, he had a notice in his garden warning visitors to beware of mantraps, and when questioned about them he would indicate his three housemaids! His cousin Charles Kingsley, the author of *The Water Babies*, stayed here with him in his country rectory, and other distinguished visitors to this eccentric man were Ruskin and the painter Turner. His hobby was woodcarving, and some of his work is in the church in which he preached for more than 50 years. He lived to be 101, and became known as the oldest parson in England.

Still in the parish of South Kilvington are the village of Upsall and Upsall Castle, some 2$\frac{1}{2}$ miles away. The village houses have many interesting architectural details. There are ornate chimneys, patterned roofs and elaborate eaves. The doorway of the old forge is in the shape of a horseshoe, with the date 1859 carved over the archway – and, elevating the status of the village, the words Upsall Town. The present Upsall Castle was built in 1924, after a fire in 1918 had destroyed the 19th century castle, which in its turn was built on the site of the 14th century home of the Scropes. They, according to tradition, had looked for buried treasure at the castle, following instructions in a dream. Two crocks of gold were discovered, but a third, supposedly buried beneath a bottery (elderberry bush), is reputed to be hidden there still.

SPOFFORTH *Grid ref. SE 365505*

When, in 1985, the field before the castle at Spofforth was threatened by the possibility of being built upon, the people and parish council of this peaceful village between Harrogate and Wetherby raised the funds and purchased it, thus preserving the green open space beside the little River Crimple. Although always referred to as Spofforth Castle, it is, strictly speaking, the impressive remains of a fortified manor house, once the home of the Percy family. The Percys were powerful in the north of England during the Middle Ages, but when they moved their base further north to Alnwick in Northumberland Spofforth became less important. Refashioned in the 14th century from an earlier castle, it was built into the solid rock on which it stands, but dismantled after the death of Sir Henry Percy at the Battle of Towton, when the Lancastrians were so bloodily defeated. The oldest part of the remains is the undercroft, dating from the close of the 12th century and accessible down a flight of rocky steps. The castle was restored in 1560 but was finally partially demolished by Cromwell, like so many elsewhere.

A long-forgotten and inferior 18th century poet, Lawrence Eusden, was baptised in the church here. Though unworthy of the honour, he became Poet Laureate in 1718 and made an enemy of Alexander Pope, who denounced him in his mock epic *The Dunciad*.

In the churchyard is the grave of one of Yorkshire's most remarkable men. Blind Jack Metcalfe was born in Knaresborough in 1717 and lost his sight at the age of six as a result of smallpox. He never let this prevent him from doing anything, running, boxing, wrestling and climbing trees like any other boy. He overcame his handicap to become a fiddler of some repute, a stage coach proprietor, a forest guide and a timber merchant. He marched all the way to the Battle of Culloden and served as a musician in the army against Bonnie Prince Charlie.

But perhaps his greatest claim to fame is as the builder of some of the best roads in Yorkshire. He designed a special instrument – his 'way-wiser' – to survey and take preliminary measurements, and this strange object can still be seen in the museum at the Old Court House in Knaresborough. A story is told how once when a thick fog descended and a traveller was grumbling at the necessity of spending the night in York, Blind Jack on overhearing him promised he could guide him safely to Harrogate through fog and forest, which he did, without mishap and in record time. Jack died in 1810 aged 93.

STAITHES *Grid ref. NZ 785185*

—— Like Robin Hood's Bay and the other coastal villages nearby, Staithes was a busy centre for smuggling. It suffered the same hardships and disasters at sea, sharing too the heroism of the local lifeboatmen. It was here that the young James Cook was apprenticed to a grocer and draper and first felt the urge to go to sea, until it became so strong that he eventually deserted his master, taking a shilling from the till according to some stories, and made his way to Whitby. The shop where he served has long since been swept away by the fury of the seas that batter this coast.

At the top of the cliff the village seems disappointingly unexceptional, but its charm is hidden in the older part down below. In the latter part of the 19th and early 20th centuries it was a centre for what came to be known as the Staithes Group – artists attracted by the rugged landscape, the picturesque effects of the red-roofed houses tumbling down the steep road to the sea, and the ready availability of models among the fishermen and their families. Probably the best known of the group is Dame Laura Knight, who lived there for 12 years at the beginning of her career. The artists were accepted into the community, providing a welcome addition to the meagre income from fishing, but were expected to respect the strict way of life there and keep the Sabbath as a day of rest. One artist seen painting on Sunday was pelted with rotten fish heads!

A regular item of wear for the women of Staithes was once the traditional bonnet, which can be seen in some of the works of Frank Meadow Sutcliffe, the famous Whitby photographer, and is still occasionally seen today, worn by the older generation – possibly for the benefit of the tourists' cameras. Modern examples can also be found in the shops, on sale as sunhats. The pattern of the bonnet is peculiar to the village and consists of a double crown and a double pleated frill, which is almost 3 inches wide at the front; it is tied at the back with a bow. The purpose of the bonnet was certainly practical rather than decorative. The women worked alongside the men, carrying the bait and the coiled fishing lines on their heads down to the boats, and the bonnets served as protection for their hair, also keeping it free of the fishy smell that was everywhere as the catch was sorted, dried and cured on the beach.

Today many of the houses in the little cobbled streets and alleys are let as holiday homes and the tourist trade is important to the village. But the lobster pots along the harbour wall are a familiar and characteristic sight, as are the fishermen often to be seen mending them. Lobster fishing has grown, reviving Staithes as a fishing port.

STILLINGFLEET *Grid ref. SE 595405*

There is a village on the B1222, some six miles or so south of York, that attracts visitors from far and wide to see its dragons and Viking boat. It is of course Stillingfleet, and the dragons and boat in question are to be found on the ironwork of the door which was once set in the fine Norman south doorway of St Helen's church. The door now stands inside the church to protect it from the weather. The hinges form a large C-shape, ending in serpent or dragon heads, and other emblems include a Viking-style longboat with a dragon-headed prow, and a pair of figures who may be Adam and Eve. These reflections of Norse tradition have led to the local belief that it was made in celebration of the victory of 1066 at Stamford Bridge, when King Harold defeated his brother Tostig and Harald Hardrada. Certainly it is the finest example of wrought iron strapwork still to be seen in its original home. There are other items worthy of note in the church. A column dividing the Moreby chapel and the nave is carved with the rare subject of a Saracen in submission. Another has a green man, the Celtic figure of fertility, his head surrounded by foliage issuing from his mouth.

In the churchyard, overlooking the road, a simple stone tells a tragic story. It marks the communal grave of nine carol singers who drowned when their boat capsized crossing the nearby River Ouse on Boxing Day 1833. Two more bodies were never recovered, but according to tradition the twelfth member of the group survived because the fiddle on his back kept him afloat.

The door in Stillingfleet church.

This unremarkable agricultural village, with its treasure of Norman architecture, found itself part of the Selby coalfield when coal was found in the 1970s. Amid much controversy, however, the pit faced closure in 2002.

STOKESLEY *Grid ref. NZ 525085*

Just within the northern boundary of North Yorkshire, with the Cleveland Hills to the south, is Stokesley, one of the many gracious old market towns to be found in the county. The roads from the surrounding countryside take one into the spacious High Street and the market place, known as The Plain – no doubt a reflection on its wide open space – where the town hall, built in 1853, takes pride of place in the centre. The town has some fine Georgian houses, old inns and an old manor house, now the library. West Green at the end of the High Street is an attractive area of trees and grass with period houses and cottages.

The River Leven flows through the town, crossed by various little bridges, including an ancient single-arched packhorse bridge from the 16th century, which is just wide enough for a packhorse to pass. It seems to have had several names over the years: Pennyman's Bridge, after an important family in the area, one of whom became the incumbent of the church in 1653; Taylerson's Bridge, from cloth merchants in the town who gave financial support for its maintenance; and, in the 19th century, Cail's Bridge, after the owners of a warehouse nearby. In July 1638 it was stated to be in a decayed state, and at the quarter sessions the townspeople were ordered to repair it 'before Michaelmas next', as the parson, whose rectory was across the river from the main part of the town, could not cross to visit the sick because of its condition.

Cross the bridge onto Levenside and continue in an easterly direction, past the old chapel, now a private house, and beyond Preston House look out for a plaque. It tells of Miss Jane Pace, who was born in Stokesley in 1817. In 1836 she became the first white woman settler in Victoria, Australia.

The parish church of St Peter and St Paul is tucked away near the river and contains some interesting items. An old coffin lid bears the unusual symbol of a pair of shears, probably relating to the cloth trade. The nave dates from the 17th century but other parts are much older, including the medieval chancel, in which lies Lady Anne Balliol, sister of the founder of Balliol College at Oxford.

STONEGRAVE *Grid ref. SE 656778*

The term minster can be applied not only to large or important ecclesiastical buildings such as the cathedrals at York and Ripon but also to parish churches, as is the case at St Gregory's Minster, Kirkdale and here at Stonegrave. Such churches are entitled to be called a minster by virtue of having once had attached to them a group of ordained monks, who served a wide area around. Stonegrave Minster stands in a quiet corner of the village looking out across the fields and open countryside. There has been a church in this tranquil spot from the very earliest times.

Fragments of stone crosses, and one almost complete one, found in the 19th century but dating from the 9th and 10th centuries, can be seen in the church. The style of the carvings on the fragments is found nowhere else in Ryedale. That of the larger cross is traditional to Iona and Galloway in Scotland. Two interesting 18th century memorials in the church could perhaps be described as wills and testaments in stone. One sets out the details of a bequest contributing to the maintenance of the fabric of the church that continues to this day. The other is a list of the members and heirs of a family, presumably intended to prevent unseemly family squabbles over inheritance claims! A medieval effigy in the church is unusual in that it shows an individual not of the knightly class whose legs are nevertheless crossed in the attitude usually reserved for a knight.

The village, on the road between Helmsley and Malton, is small but attractive. It lies at the foot of the Hambletons under the wooded slope of Caulkley's Bank, with cottages tucked up against rock faces. It was here that Sir Herbert Read, the writer, art critic, philosopher and poet, returning to his roots, spent the last years of his life. He was born at Kirkbymoorside into a family of yeomen farmers and spent his early years on the farm. He is buried at St Gregory's Minster, where he worshipped in his youth.

SUTTON BANK *Grid ref. SE 515825*

▬▬▬ The traveller on the A170 road from Helmsley to Thirsk should pause at the top of the notorious Sutton Bank, 1,000 feet above sea level, for one of England's truly magnificent views. On a clear day, an enormous area of Yorkshire is visible across the plain of York and as far as the distant Pennines. To the left it is possible to walk past the gliding club to the white horse carved in the hillside, and to the right down to Lake Gormire, one of Yorkshire's few natural lakes.

It was claimed for many years that the lake was bottomless, but soundings carried out in the 1930s found that its greatest depth was only 21 feet. The myth of a gigantic pike in its waters was also disproved at the same time, but the mystery of where the waters come from or where they go to remains. Springs in the depths have been suggested as the source, and it has been noticed that when the lake is full a small stream runs from it into the rocks of the escarpment rising on its eastern bank. Like Hodge Beck at Kirkdale, it is said to come out at Kirkbymoorside, and we find the same legend of the disappearing duck – though this one is reputed to have arrived at its distant destination stripped of all its feathers!

The 1,500 yard drive down Sutton Bank, with its gradients of 1 in 5 and 1 in 4 and a Z-bend in the middle, is an experience not to be missed, not least because of the breathtaking views. In the days of the horse it needed as many as five or six to haul a wagon to the top, and in the early days of motorised horsepower even the motorcar was sometimes defeated. In severe winter weather the road can still become impassable. In 1755 John Wesley recorded in his journal the thunderous fall of huge masses of rock to the bottom of the cliff. Today, however, regular checks and precautions forestall any such problems on the road.

TADCASTER *Grid ref. SE 486432*

▬▬▬ The smell of hops and beer wafting over the town is a familiar one in Tadcaster, where brewing has long been the town's most important industry, providing many jobs for the area.

Tadcaster has a very long history. It was important in Roman times as *Calcaria*, an outpost of the military station of *Eboracum* (York), and coins and pottery have been found here, as well as traces of the actual camp.

The town has been subject to flooding from time to time, and the parish church, dating mostly from the 15th century but with earlier parts too, was moved in the 19th century to its present position away from the area at risk from the River Wharfe. The old many-arched bridge over the river is said to contain stone from a castle that once stood nearby.

That may or may not be so, but more certain is the fact that limestone from a particular quarry near Tadcaster named Jackdaw Crag quarry has provided stone for York Minster down the centuries. Its former name of Peter's Post links it with the Minster, which is dedicated to St Peter. The quarry, together with others, belonged to the Catholic Vavasour family of Hazlewood Castle (now a hotel and restaurant), who, during Protestant Elizabethan times, enjoyed the rare privilege of being allowed to celebrate Mass in their private chapel, free of hindrance or persecution. This was said to be as a reward for freely giving their stone to the minster and other churches.

There were those who claimed it was due to the influence of Anne Vavasour, who was Queen Elizabeth's favourite maid-of-honour, while others thought it was likely to be because Sir Thomas Vavasour commanded a ship which took part in the successful rout of the Spanish Armada. But surely the figure of Sir William Vavasour holding a block of stone stands in a niche beside the west door of York Minster as the ultimate honour for his contribution to its fabric?

Various plans for the now disused quarry have been put forward, one interesting and ambitious suggestion being to flood it and make a lake to provide recreational facilities for residents and visitors.

TAN HILL *Grid ref. NY 895065*

——— England's highest public house stands 1,732 feet above sea level, on exposed and desolate moorland on the northern edge of the Yorkshire Dales National Park. Dating from the 18th century, the Tan Hill Inn owes its existence to the coal pits and lead mines that once surrounded it, and whose workers it served. Coal was dug in the area from as early as the 13th century and Tan Hill was at the centre of the routes and pack horse tracks that ran to and from the pits. The road from Reeth to Tan Hill was made a turnpike road in 1741, and by the end of the 19th century as many as 60 carts might be seen on an autumn day, arriving at the pits to fetch coal for the winter. By the early 1930s, however, the Tan Hill colliery had become the last of them to close.

An eccentric character from the days of the coalmines was George Kearton of nearby Oxnop Hall, who employed an army of miners and provided them with gallons of ale. He fought as a wrestler at contests at Tan Hill, rode to hounds in a pony chaise at the age of 100 and died in 1764, aged 125.

The coming of the motor car has meant that Tan Hill Inn has lost some of its remoteness, but it still stands alone in a bleak landscape; the nearest village, Keld, is 4½ miles away in Swaledale. It is not unknown for people to be stranded here in bad weather. There is a story that once the landlord had been to Richmond to apply for his annual licence but, realising that his hours had not been specified, he hurried back, only to be told: 'You have permission to keep open day and night. Refuse no one at Tan Hill.' It would surely take a hard heart to turn anyone away in distress on this bleak moor!

THIRSK *Grid ref. SE 430822*

—— Many people come to this busy and historic market town to see the fictional Darrowby of the James Herriot books and the popular television series *All Creatures Great and Small*. Alf Wight, the author of the books, lived and had his practice here and based his stories on his experiences in the area.

The very large cobbled market square, with its unusual clock tower and its bull ring, is surrounded by old houses, shops and inns. Some, like the Golden Fleece, are old coaching inns from the time when the town was a famous posting stage. The old market cross has been removed from the square to the grounds of Thirsk Hall, which was built in the 18th century near the magnificent early-15th century parish church of St Mary. Nothing but the site remains of the Norman castle built beside Cod Beck by Roger de Mowbray. It was demolished after its surrender to the king, following the failure of the rebellion against Henry II.

Fans of Alf Wight's books can now visit the house in Kirkgate, just off the market square, where he lived and in which he had his veterinary surgery. It is now a museum, reconstructed and refurnished to be exactly as it was when he began in veterinary practice.

His is not the only name to be remembered, however, in this small town. Also in Kirkgate, almost opposite the Herriot Museum and also a museum, is the little house where on November 23rd 1755 Thomas Lord was born. Though the son of a poor labourer, he was to become the founder of Lord's Cricket Ground, the headquarters of the Marylebone Cricket Club in London. In 1780 he was groundsman at the White Conduit Club in London and later had charge of a cricket ground for the Earl of Winchester. In 1787 he started a ground of his own on what is now Dorset Square, then moved close to the Regent's Canal and finally in 1814 to the present site, which still bears his name.

Nor does the town's contribution to the game of cricket end there. George Gibson Macaulay (1897–1940), the Yorkshire and England player, was born here, and Maurice Leyland (1900–1967), the lefthander, who also played for Yorkshire and England, had connections with Thirsk.

The cricket memorabilia in one small room in Lord's birthplace will be of interest to lovers of the sport, but there are other items of general interest. One particular exhibit, a Windsor chair, known as the Busby Stoop chair after the name of the inn from which it came, has a fearful superstition attached to it. Once the favourite chair in the inn of a man hanged in 1702 for clipping coins, it is said that anyone who sits in it will shortly die, that fate having befallen two customers who used it after his death. I am glad to say that the chair is roped off, lest anyone should be brave – or foolhardy – enough to decide to test the truth of the superstition.

Should you wonder about the meaning of the emblem on the little museum's sign, the answer lies in the history of the area. Seek out the unique old milestone in Ingramgate and you will see the same figure on it. It is that of a drover with stick in one hand and beer in the other. The driving of cattle from Scotland and the north reached a peak in the 19th century when a million or more were driven in one year along the ancient drovers' road

The unique milestone, Ingramgate, Thirsk.

across the nearby Hambleton Hills to market at York, and even as far beyond as Smithfield in London. Thirsk must have been a popular stopping place for the drovers, not only for its market, but also for the three Rs – rest, refreshment and recreation.

THOLTHORPE *Grid ref. SE 474668*

The little village of Tholthorpe, a few miles south-west of Easingwold, encircles a large village green and an attractive duck pond, fringed by reeds and weeping trees making an idyllic rural scene. But at times when the sun is shining strongly a strange sight can be seen. The water of the pond turns blood red. This is no tale, for I have seen for myself this unusual phenomenon. According to the experts, it is caused not by some uncanny magic but by rich nutrients in the water feeding an alga, *Eugleana sanguena*, which is affected by strong sunlight, turning it from green to red.

In 1939 land here was requisitioned by the Air Ministry, and this quiet little village became the temporary home, throughout the war, of Canadian airmen stationed at the airfield that was built nearby. In 1986 a simple Canadian granite memorial, inscribed in both English and French, was erected on the village green to commemorate those men, and English oaks and Canadian maples were planted along both sides of the road leading to the airfield. The airfield itself has since been put to rural industrial use, but this small corner of North Yorkshire has become a place of pilgrimage for Canadian veterans, their relatives and other visitors.

THORNTON LE DALE *Grid ref. SE 831830*

Is it Thornton le Dale or simply Thornton Dale? The village, the first of several strung out along the road between the towns of Pickering and Scarborough, has been known at different times by first one and then the other name, and both can still be heard. It was a settlement long before 1086, the time of the Domesday Book, and was recorded therein as *Torentune*. Whatever name is used, it can be said with certainty that it is one of the most delightful villages in Yorkshire.

Its reputation as the prettiest village (though challenged by others in the county) has proved to be a mixed blessing, bringing throngs of trippers and visitors with their coaches and cars. The attractions of the village make it an ideal place to take a break on the journey to Scarborough or Whitby, and the cafés and gift shops, which have developed as a result over the years, are a popular draw. It can get very crowded with both people and traffic.

It is easy to see what brings the crowds. On the village green is the ancient market cross, where in medieval times the Abbot of Whitby paid annual tribute in large amounts of herrings to the hospital of St Leonard in York. Nearby are the old village stocks. The shallow Thornton Beck ripples over a stony bed through the village street and little bridges cross it to the pretty cottages in their colourful gardens. Trout can be seen in the beck, and the pond near the village car park is a haven for ducks and wild waterfowl. Both trout-spotting and feeding the ducks give pleasure to many children, and not a few adults.

Along one side of the main street are twelve 17th century almshouses and beyond that a small building of 1657, once a grammar school for the classical education of local boys. The almshouses and school were both founded by Lady Lumley of Thornton and Sinnington, whose name is now given to the school in Pickering. A fine row of chestnut trees once stood before the almshouses but was sadly sacrificed to the needs of the motor car.

Where the beck turns at the top of the street is the much-photographed thatched cottage, Beck Isle Cottage, dating from the 16th century. It has appeared many times, not only in visitors' photograph albums, but also on chocolate boxes, calendars and jigsaws.

All Saints' church, first built in the 14th century, stands on a high bank facing down the village street. In the churchyard is the gravestone of Matthew Grimes, who died in 1875 at the great age of 96. As a soldier he had guarded Napoleon in exile on St Helena and was one of the bearers of his coffin when he died.

Thornton le Dale welcomes its visitors warmly but has not always depended on the tourist trade for its daily bread. There were many different industries there in the past: corn milling, quarrying, shoemaking, weaving and tailoring. Less than a mile away, in the hamlet of Ellerburn, the making of paper and fish-farming are remembered in the names Paper Mill Farm and Fishponds. Nothing remains of Roxby Castle, the home of the Cholmley family in the time of Elizabeth I, except a few grassy mounds, but the name lives on in Roxby Road.

I have been told that a less desirable address was given at the end of the 19th and beginning of the 20th century to dwellings at the 'backside' of the house of one Betty Walker. But perhaps you should be left to work that one out for yourselves!

THWAITE *Grid ref. SD 893985*

The road from Hawes in Wensleydale crosses over into Swaledale through the Buttertubs Pass and drops down into Thwaite. In a terrible storm in 1898, the village suffered great damage and was almost washed away by a flood down the fellside. Today there is little to remind one of the disaster among its neat grey stone cottages, field barns and dry stone walling – all very typical of the Dales landscape.

It was here, in a tiny cottage, that the brothers Cherry (1871–1940) and Richard (1862–1928) Kearton were born. The sons of a gamekeeper and shepherd, they were to become well-known naturalists and authors. They went to school at Muker, a mile away, Cherry riding a penny-farthing bicycle and Richard, who was lame, making his way on foot, and they gained their knowledge of nature from the countryside around them. It was Cherry who devised and developed the technique of taking wildlife photographs from a hide – a novel idea at the time. Both brothers learned from an early age to imitate the calls of most of the creatures of the surrounding countryside, using them to attract their subjects. Many people first found out about such places as Thwaite, Muker and Buttertubs Pass, and their flora, and fauna from the brothers' books and Cherry's broadcasts and his autobiographical film.

The little village is proud of its connection with the Kearton brothers, and the local guesthouse and restaurant, where one can enjoy a typical old-fashioned Yorkshire high tea, bears their name.

TOWTON *Grid ref. SE 485395*

Every year on Palm Sunday, barring such unpredictable events as the foot-and-mouth restrictions of 2001, members of the Towton Battlefield Society walk over the battleground and place a wreath of red and white roses at the foot of a stone cross in a field beside the road to Saxton, south of Tadcaster. It is their way of commemorating the 28,000 or more men who died there on Palm Sunday 1461 in the largest and most bloody battle of the Wars of the Roses. In a blinding snowstorm, the two armies clashed for ten hours until corpses were strewn for six miles over the battlefield. When the Lancastrians finally tried to flee, no quarter was given in vicious hand-to-hand fighting. The Yorkists drove them down to Cock Beck, where their bodies blocked the stream, which ran red with their blood.

A battle grave of 40 men, recently discovered during building work in the village of Towton, has revealed just how savage was medieval warfare. Modern scientific study of their injuries shows how they were repeatedly hacked around the head, in some cases when they were felled to the ground or already dead; 113 wounds were noted on just 27 of the skulls. It was also possible to learn from their wounds the types of weapons used, including poleaxes, hammers and swords, as well as arrows. Some of the bodies had evidence of earlier wounds that had healed, suggesting that they were veteran soldiers, and their unexpectedly tall and athletic build could have meant that they were members of an elite corps.

The little church at Lead, standing isolated in a field today, supposedly sheltered the wounded, and scores of dead are said to be buried nearby. This unremarkable agricultural land around Saxton and Towton once saw hideous sights, belied by its quietness today, the quietness of the untold dead who lie beneath it. In the churchyard at Saxton is the tomb of Lord Dacre, a Lancastrian, said to have been shot by a boy in a tree when he took off his helmet to drink a cup of wine. According to tradition, he was buried in an upright position together with his horse, though I have been unable to find a reason for such an unorthodox burial.

WELL *Grid ref. SE 265895*

The village of Well, between Ripon and Bedale, owes its simple name to a well, which the early Christians declared holy and dedicated to St Michael. It is one of several springs feeding the stream that flows through the village. The well would have been known to the Romans, for remains of a villa and bathhouse have been excavated here. A section of tessellated pavement from the villa is now in Well church.

In feudal times, much of North Yorkshire was owned by a few powerful families, such as the Nevilles of Middleham and Sheriff Hutton, and the Latimers of Danby, Snape and Well, who were connected by marriage. Ralph Neville of Middleham built the church of St Michael the Archangel at Well, around 1350, and in 1342 founded the Hospital of St Michael for 24 men and women, 'needy poor persons', known as bedesmen and bedeswomen, in the care of a chaplain and two priests. At a later date Richard III, who had married Anne Neville, the younger daughter of Richard Neville (Warwick the Kingmaker), was to become its patron. King Richard, who has been portrayed as an infamous and ruthless man, was always popular and well loved in Yorkshire, and still has his supporters to this day, who feel that he has been very much maligned. The hospital was eventually acquired by Robert de Tateshall for his personal use, and almshouses, now called St Michael's Cottages, were built near the church. The north wing of Well Hall, containing a magnificent stone vaulted chamber with pillars down the centre, was the original hospital.

In the church there are memorials to various Nevilles and Latimers, amongst them Sir John Neville, the last Lord Latimer. His father had three wives, one of whom was Catherine Parr, who lived at nearby Snape Castle. She became the sixth and last wife of Henry VIII, having the good fortune to outlive him.

WENSLEY *Grid ref. SE 093895*

Wensleydale, with its numerous waterfalls and bold escarpments, is considered by many to be the loveliest of all the Yorkshire dales. The fact that the little village of Wensley has given its name to what is certainly the largest of the dales leads one to suppose that perhaps it was once a more important place, and such is indeed the case. Until the Great Plague struck in the 16th century, it was the most important market town in the dale. Hundreds of the inhabitants died from the disease, and many others fled to Leyburn, 2 miles away, thinking it a healthier place as further from the river. Leyburn grew and was granted a charter, while Wensley never recovered from its loss of population and diminished to the size and status of a village. The church and the bridge over the River Ure are the only remains from its medieval past.

In 1678 Lord Bolton moved out of Bolton Castle, where once Mary, Queen of Scots had been imprisoned, and built for himself Bolton Hall, which then became the family seat. It is a striking building, approached from Wensley village through extensive parkland and set against the background of Redmire Woods. It was rebuilt in 1902 after it was partially destroyed by fire.

Charles Paulet, 1st Duke of Bolton, was an eccentric who turned night into day, sleeping during the day and entertaining through the night. He refused to speak at all until late in the day because he thought the air then was purer. In Holy Trinity church, the Bolton family pews have a distinctly theatrical appearance, though not surprisingly, since they are two opera boxes, removed in the 18th century from Drury Lane Theatre when it was undergoing refurbishment. The duke had fallen in love with the singer who took the part of Polly Peachum in *The Beggar's Opera*. She was his mistress for many years until he married her on the death of his wife. It seems, however, that perhaps the charms of an operatic mistress do not carry over into married life, for it is said that a tower, known as Polly Peachum's Tower, was built by the duke as a place in which she could sing when he could no longer bear to listen to her!

Wensley today is an unspoilt agricultural village, attracting visitors to its craft centre and the beautiful surrounding countryside.

WESTERDALE   *Grid ref. NZ 665065*

High on Westerdale Moor are the remains of an Iron Age settlement, crowned by a circular enclosure. Through the ages many tales have been told of battles fought between the Romans and the Ancient Britons in this area, known as Crown End. The River Esk also rises on Westerdale Moor, at the head of the valley where the small streams known as the Esklets unite. It runs down the dale before turning eastward at Castleton to enter the sea at Whitby. West of Castleton is the little village of Westerdale, surrounded by wild open spaces and tranquillity.

On the northern edge of the village is Westerdale Hall, standing on what is thought to have been a site of the Knights Hospitallers in the 16th century. Now a youth hostel, it was built in the 1840s in the Scottish baronial style as a shooting lodge for the Duncombe family of the Feversham estate. Below the hall, the Esk is crossed by a packhorse bridge bearing the Duncombe coronet and a restoration tablet from 1874. The name Hunter's-Stee, referring to the steep road leading from the bridge down into the village, is applied locally to the bridge itself.

In the village, in the garden of a cottage named Arkangel, is a large grey stone pillar telling a dramatic story of shipwreck and escape from death. It is the work of Thomas Bulmer, who retired from the sea to live in this cottage in Westerdale. Four boats are carved on the base and almost every inch of the pillar is covered with inscriptions, which seem to be both a thanksgiving to God and a reminder of man's mortality. The date 1727 is followed by the words 'In this year it was my true intent to make here a lasting monument to show Thy mercies everywhere abound and save us when no mankind are to be found. Of this I have had large expieryance.' He then goes on to describe the circumstances of his 'expieryance' of God's mercy during his journeys across the seas. He tells us first of the many foreign shores that he has been to, and continues: 'Wrecked at length his frail bark the hopeful anchors cast is now unrigged and here lyeth moored fast. Tossed on rough seas on broken pieces of the ship until daybreak when they escaped all safe to land. Remember man thy sail on sea short it must be and then returned to dust.'

With its solemn but somewhat incoherent and ambiguous words, this old stone pillar is a powerful inspiration to the imagination and arouses a desire to know more about Thomas Bulmer. His gravestone stands against the rear wall of Westerdale church, and next to it is that of a boy aged only 17, also named Bulmer. Like the monument in the cottage garden, it is dated 1727. The placing of the two stones together leads one to wonder whether the boy was Thomas's son. But sadly the stones are barely decipherable and cannot tell us more.

WEST SCRAFTON *Grid ref. SE 075836*

——— The Aire, the Ribble, the Swale, the Ure and the Wharfe are the five principal rivers whose valleys form the Yorkshire Dales, but there are numerous smaller rivers branching off in smaller dales. Coverdale (pronounced to rhyme with hover) is one of these. Miles Coverdale (1488–1569), the translator of the first published version of the complete Bible in English, was born in this lonely dale, from which he takes his name. West Scrafton is one of the few villages in the dale. The River Cover runs below it, with ancient terraced arable fields between. Open common stretches to Roova Crags and beyond are Carlton Moor and Penhill, the lair of a legendary giant who ravaged and terrorised the countryside.

A long disused mine on West Scrafton Moor produced coal of such poor quality that it earned the local name Scrafton Crackers, owing to its propensity to crack and spit out tiny bits. It would no doubt be the cause of many tiny holes burnt into the clipped rag hearth rugs that were common once in rural Yorkshire and are now gaining popularity again as a rural craft. On winter evenings, when a new rug was needed, the whole family would work around a wooden frame on which a piece of hessian was stretched; the children were allowed to cut the 'clips' and the adults pricked them into the hessian with a simple wooden prodder.

West Scrafton clusters around an unusually tiny village green and is built over a huge pot (cavern). The stream which runs underground in the pot for more than a mile enters the River Cover from a cave known as Otter's Hole. Nearby is Tom Hunter's Parlour, a cave where a highwayman who robbed travellers on the road from London, hid his loot and was eventually arrested.

WEST TANFIELD *Grid ref. SE 269788*

The village of West Tanfield is situated in varied and beautiful scenery, about three miles south-east of Masham, on the northern bank of the River Ure. An old three-arched stone bridge crosses the river, and nearby are the church and a 15th century gatehouse with an oriel window over its entrance.

Known as the Marmion Tower, it is all that remains of the castle of the Marmion family, who first came here in 1215 and figured prominently in the wars of the first three kings named Edward. One member of the family who particularly distinguished himself may have been the inspiration for the hero of Sir Walter Scott's great romantic poem *Marmion*. John, Lord Marmion was granted permission by Edward II to castellate his manor house as reward for his services in fighting the Scots. The only visible remnant, the gatehouse, was probably built by Elizabeth Marmion's husband, Henry Fitzhugh, and its history is not known. When the castle was destroyed, the stones and materials are reputed to have been purchased by neighbouring gentry and used to build their own halls.

The village church of St Nicholas contains the Marmion tombs, as well as some beautiful woodwork carved with figures and animals, monks playing musical instruments and St Nicholas with three children in a tub. The mouse of Robert Thompson of Kilburn is also to be found lurking here. The church has two interesting architectural details, namely, a small bay projecting into the churchyard from the nave and a tiny chamber by the chancel arch.

In June 1871 Elizabeth Clarke of Tanfield House married a soldier with the splendid name of Colonel Rookes Evelyn Bell Crompton. Her parents' house became the first in England to have electricity from water power, when Colonel Crompton sited a waterwheel between an island in the Ure and the bank to drive a generator which provided the energy. As the head of a great commercial enterprise, he went on to provide lighting for both Buckingham Palace and Windsor Castle.

WEST WITTON   *Grid ref. SE 064881*

West Witton is a long ribbon village of grey houses, under Penhill, on the road between Leyburn and Aysgarth. Appropriately for this village in the very heart of Wensleydale, the local pub bears the name of The Wensleydale Heifer; the sign is a picture of an old-fashioned brown and white prize beast, although today most of the cattle that one sees in the area are black and white Friesians.

Like many villages, West Witton has its feast day, held on the weekend nearest to 24th August, the feast of St Bartholomew, to whom the village church is dedicated. Today the feast is a one-day event, but the Victorians celebrated for three whole days, with stalls lining the village street and flares lighting it at night. There were fairings for the adults and sweets for the children. Races were run, with copper kettles for prizes, and the main event was a dog trail. Dances were held at the inn, and families and friends gathered to enjoy a huge joint of meat referred to as a 'lump o' Bartle'. Even up to the Second World War the celebrations included a real feast, which traditionally involved the consumption of Yorkshire curd cheesecakes. That particular tradition, it seems, has expired but an unusual custom – the 'burning of Bartle' – is still kept alive as a finale to the day's festivities.

It involves the carrying of an effigy along the village street and the reciting of a verse, which seems to refer to a chase of some kind, at various points along the way. No one knows the origin of this curious custom. It has been suggested that it may be linked with a legend of a wicked giant of Penhill, or be an ancient fertility rite associated with the harvest. Certainly the 'burning of Bartle' does not have any connection with burning the saint but takes its name solely from the association with St Bartholomew's day.

WHARRAM PERCY *Grid ref. SE 855645*

Although there are signposts pointing the way to Wharram Percy on the B1248 from Malton to Beverley, this village south-east of Malton in a valley of the Wolds is no ordinary village. It is the best preserved of the many lost medieval villages, which were abandoned for various reasons at different times. Many were deserted after the Black Death had all but wiped out their population. Wharram Percy, though affected, was not one of these, but was a victim of the growth in the woollen cloth industry. This brought about a shift from arable to sheep farming, which, needing only a handful of workers, was more profitable for landowners than letting out the land in small parcels to be cultivated by the peasantry. The many villagers who were dispossessed were forced to seek a livelihood elsewhere. By 1435 the village was reduced from 30 houses to 16 and totally deserted by the end of the century.

The church survived and continued to be used by the people from the nearby village of Thixendale until the 19th century, when they built their own. Although it is now a roofless ruin, it is still the venue of an annual service. Today nothing but the ground plans of the houses can be seen. No one lives here and to the unimaginative eye it consists only of bumps and hollows yet in a sense Wharram Percy is far from deserted. Over more than 40 years, archaeologists excavated the site, gaining from it much historical knowledge and learning new archaeological techniques. The site is an English Heritage property, open all year round, and many visitors and students make the journey from the village of Wharram-le-Street down the narrow road to Wharram Percy car park to walk along the medieval roadway to Wharram Percy itself.

Standing in this village which is no more, one reflects on the community which no doubt expected it to continue on that spot for all time and yet had to uproot itself and disperse to find a life elsewhere.

Not far from here, the water of the Gypsey Race rises near Duggleby and makes its way, often underground, through the Great Wold Valley to the coast at Bridlington, where it runs into the harbour. Its name derives from the Old Norse word *gypa* 'spring' and it behaves in an erratic manner – sometimes disappearing for years at a time, only to bubble forth again. As a result, there is a superstition that when it flows it heralds some great disaster and it has acquired the name Woe Waters. Since at any given time a disaster is occurring somewhere, no doubt there has been much 'proof' of its truth over the years! The more boring view is that the porous nature of the chalkland and the height of the water table might just be involved.

WHITBY *Grid ref. NZ 896108*

Approaching across the North York Moors from Pickering and into the town by Downdinner Hill adds a special pleasure, but from whichever direction one arrives Whitby is a matchless delight. Not just a holiday resort but also a fishing port, it has quaint streets, where one can buy Whitby jet and Whitby kippers, stately Georgian terraces, a harbour and pier, lighthouses and the famous lifeboat. There are cliffs and sands, quays busy with the excitement of an early morning fish auction, and the best fish and chips in the country at the black and white Magpie Restaurant on Pier Road. Whitby has associations important not just to Yorkshire but also to the country as a whole. It was here in AD 664, at the abbey high above the town on the east cliff, that the question of when Easter should be celebrated was resolved and the Roman way of Christianity was adopted. It was here that England's first poet, the humble 7th century herdsman Caedmon, discovered his gift, and it was from here that Captain Cook set sail on his voyages of discovery. Look out for his ship, the *Endeavour*, on a weathervane not far from his statue on the west cliff.

William Scoresby and his son brought prosperity to the town with the whaling industry; William also invented the crow's nest look-out on ships. He and his son, and all who worked in the whaling industry, are commemorated with a whalebone arch, also on West Cliff. This was brought over from Alaska to replace a previous one, which had deteriorated dangerously.

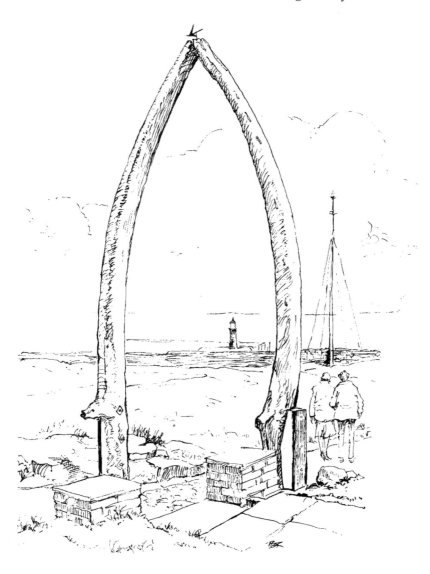

The whalebone arch, Whitby.

It will be noticed, incidentally, that Whitby has east and west cliffs, while Scarborough's cliffs, only 20 miles away, are north and south. This is due to Whitby's northern orientation as a result of which it is possible to see a strange phenomenon here during the two weeks before and after the summer solstice (21st June): the sun both rising and setting over the sea.

Just below the abbey ruins, on the eroding cliff high above the sea, the church of St Mary has been reached from as early as 1370 by a stairway, originally of wood, but replaced by stone between 1750 and 1770. The number of steps has varied over the years, but since the 1830s the many visitors who have counted them as they climbed will have found that there are 199. A yearly event was a race up and down the steps, which when revived in 1977 was won in 32 seconds. Those panting their way up more slowly may be grateful for the benches on the flat areas at intervals along the way, unaware that they were originally intended as rests for coffins being carried up to the church.

The interior of the church is like no other. Able to seat 2,000, it is a jumble of galleries, pillars and box pews, some individually reserved, others marked 'Strangers Only'. Behind the three-tiered pulpit, which was fitted with amplifying tubes for the benefit of the deaf wife of one of the vicars, is a so-called jade's pew, of which there are very few surviving examples. It was reserved for the public humiliation of any woman found guilty of adultery. Seated there after walking barefoot and dressed in a shroud-like garment through the congregation, she would have to listen to a sermon calling for her to repent. No acknowledgement seems to have been made of the fact that it takes two!

Appropriately for Whitby, with its shipbuilding and seagoing traditions, the impression inside the church is of being below decks in an old sailing ship, the clerestory windows having been constructed to resemble ships' cabin windows when they were replaced in the 17th century by local ships' carpenters.

Behind the church, don't miss the memorial in a niche beside the private entrance to the Chomley family pew. It celebrates Francis and Mary Huntrodd who were born on the same day in 1600; they married on their birthday, and they died on their eightieth birthday within five hours of each other.

WYKEHAM *Grid ref. SE 965835*

Wykeham Abbey is not as one might suppose the building of a religious order but a large house set in attractive parkland. It is the seat of Viscount Downe, the Irish title having been borne by the Yorkshire Dawnay family since 1680. The house takes its name from the fact that it occupies the site of a 12th century Cistercian priory for nuns. A broken wall and a few stones are almost all that now remains of the priory, which was destroyed by fire. The estate is the largest employer in the area, with farmland, a 100-acre tree nursery and a caravan park.

Wykeham is one of a string of villages on the Pickering to Scarborough road along the edge of the moors. The visitor who pauses in this pleasant village on the way to the coast cannot fail to notice that there is a most unusual entrance to the churchyard. It is not surprising if one should think that it looks like a medieval church tower – complete with church clock and traditional weather vane – for that is exactly what it is. When All Saints' church was built in the 19th century, the tower of the chapel of St Mary and St Helen, built in the 14th century by John de Wykeham but having fallen into disrepair, was restored to serve as this unique and imposing lychgate. This has led to an amusing story of quarrelling sisters. In this fanciful tale, they decided to build a church but, when they could not agree, one built the tower and the other built the church. Nonsense, of course, but a neat idea!

YOCKENTHWAITE *Grid ref. SD 905790*

The forest where Eogan the Celt made his thwaite (from Old Norse *thveit* 'clearing') is long gone but the little hamlet of Yockenthwaite in Langstrothdale remains. Even today this is a wild part of Wharfedale, though no longer so remote and inaccessible, and it is popular with both walkers and motorists. The River Wharfe runs through the dale on its bed of limestone, with little waterfalls and shallow pools, and its banks, often only a few yards from the road, seem made for picnics or just enjoying the country air. Yockenthwaite packhorse bridge crosses it against a background of trees.

A little way to the west of Yockenthwaite, beside the River Wharfe, a circle consisting of 20 stones laid edge to edge tells us that Bronze Age man once lived in this area. The stones are not standing stones and are generally considered to be the kerbstones of a tomb. Bronze Age people settled on the valley sides where there were few trees, and on the higher limestone terraces. They have left a richness of archaeological remains, particularly in their barrows or burial mounds, which are found throughout the Dales.

YORK *Grid ref. SE 604514*

As a city with a long and interesting history, York is a treasure trove of interest. Its historic buildings and ancient connections are well known and well documented. George VI declared that 'the history of York is the history of England'. It has also been described as the city where 'streets are gates, gates are bars, and bars are pubs', and it would be difficult to think of York without its bars and city walls.

Visitors enjoying the walk on the walls, which almost completely surround the ancient city, may not realise that they have to thank the York-born artist William Etty RA for the fact that they are able to do so. When the city fathers in the 1800s had plans to demolish the walls, Etty, who never lost his love of his native city, helped to organise a successful protest group, and indeed paid from his own pocket towards the maintenance of Bootham Bar. He was also a foremost advocate of the total restoration of York Minster when it was devastated by fire in 1829 and again in 1840. His statue, somewhat weather-worn today, stands in Exhibition Square, outside the City Art Gallery, which contains many of his works. His tomb can be seen in St Olave's churchyard through an arch of the ruins of St Mary's Abbey in the Museum Gardens.

No visit to the city would be complete, of course, without a visit to its magnificent minster. Its great glory is its medieval stained glass windows. Nearly half of all the medieval glass in Britain is in the minster's 117 windows. The great East Window, the size of a tennis court, and the famous Five Sisters Window of grisaille glass cannot be missed. But do look out for the monkeys in the detail of the fifth window from west to east in the north

A monkey doctor, York Minster.

aisle. Humorous and grotesque motifs were popular in medieval times and are well represented here. One can see monkey doctors holding flasks and jars. Sadly their ministrations seem to have been in vain – for the monkey's funeral is also depicted. Other animals, a woman beating her husband, and a wrestling match are also to be seen in this window, and in the next window monkeys appear once again, this time playing musical instruments.

Also renowned for its 14th and 15th century stained glass, among the finest in York and indeed in Europe, is All Saints' church in North Street. There, in the south wall of the church, the Angels Window contains an interesting detail not to be missed. Among the figures in the bottom right-hand panel is a man wearing glasses. Although lenses were known to the ancient Greeks and in ancient China, eyeglasses were not in use until the 13th century and only became more general in the 15th century, when the glass in this window was made. They would be a new but sufficiently recognisable motif at that time for the artist to incorporate into the design, with perhaps a touch of humour, as the little face behind the large glasses peers round from behind the larger figures.

Attached to the church is a tiny hermit's cell or anchorage. It was built in the early 1900s for the then incumbent, who installed a religious recluse in it. The little building appears to have many wooden beams in its construction, but in fact they are made of concrete. A peephole or squint enabled the occupant to look down along the church to the altar. In the 1960s a young female student at York University was the last person to occupy the cell, which then fell into some disrepair, before being restored by York Civic Trust in 1987. It is no longer occupied today.

Tea and cakes in Betty's Tearooms in the centre of York is a must for visitors. During World War II Betty's Bar – entered down steps from the street above and so familiarly known as the Dive – was a favourite haunt of Canadian airmen from the many airfields around the city. Someone scratched his name on a mirror in the bar and soon others followed suit. Today, though the Dive is no more, the mirror with the names of those young men, many of whom lost their lives, can still be seen downstairs in the tearooms.

The River Ouse, which flows through the city, has always been important to its history, but for many centuries the only bridge crossing the river was Ouse Bridge. In 1154, the wooden bridge collapsed under the weight of a huge crowd which had gathered to greet their new archbishop. Men, women and children were thrown into the water, but by good fortune no one was drowned. A chapel was erected on the rebuilt bridge as an act of thanksgiving; this was common practice at the time, and travellers prayed there for their safety and protection. In the 14th and 15th centuries Ouse Bridge had so many houses and shops on it that in 1564 it again collapsed into the river, and twelve lives were lost. The foundations of the present bridge were laid in 1810 but it took ten years to complete the bridge.

Both Lendal and Skeldergate bridges were also built in the 19th century. George Hudson, York's railway king, first proposed a bridge to give more direct access to his railway station within the city walls, but it was only after years of debate and delay that Lendal Bridge was started in 1860. A terrible accident occurred, toppling the whole structure and causing five deaths and many injured. A new engineer and fresh plans were sought, and in January 1863 the cast-iron bridge was finally opened. Among its decorations of shields and angels it is said that one of the latter, looking out over the water, has the face of Queen Alexandra. (See what you think!)

Skeldergate Bridge was opened 18 years later, in January 1881. Both were toll bridges, and the toll houses still exist. The toll for a pedestrian to cross was a halfpenny, for an animal one penny and for a horse-drawn vehicle twopence. The charges may seem small to us today, but were not so small in those days and they must have added up considerably for all but the complete stay-at-home. Today we can cross from one side of York to the other almost unaware of the river, or of what a barrier it once was.

YOULTON   *Grid ref. SE 490634*

It may be just a handful of scattered houses and farms but little Youlton once played host to King James I as he travelled between London and Edinburgh. He is reputed to have slept at Youlton Hall, now a farm, but once the ancestral home of the Ellerker family. A member of this family, a Lady Ellerker, built the 14th century chapel at St Mary's church in the nearby village of Alne, in which her stone effigy lies.

A feature of the hall is a secret hiding place in a chimney; it was probably used as a priest hole at the time when Catholics followed their faith at their peril and any priest found saying the Mass could forfeit his life. There are also tales of secret underground passages from the hall to the village of Alne, supposedly used by monks in the 10th century. Such stories I think must be taken with a very large pinch of salt, given the distance between the two villages, plus the fact that the River Kyle intersects the route.

INDEX